REMEDIAL PROCESS FOR CONTAMINATED LAND

Edited by Malcolm Pratt

INSTITUTION OF CHEMICAL ENGINEERS

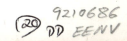

Opinions expressed in this volume are those of
the individual authors and not necessarily those
of the Institution of Chemical Engineers.

Published by
Institution of Chemical Engineers,
Davis Building,
165–171 Railway Terrace,
Rugby, Warwickshire CV21 3HQ, UK

Printed in England by Chameleon Press Ltd, 5–25 Burr Road, London SW18 4SG

PREFACE

Contaminated land is one of the legacies of past and present industrialization and waste disposal activity. Increased environmental awareness and concerns regarding the environmental impact of this contamination has resulted in the need either to remove the contaminating materials or to render them harmless. Historically, most sites in the United Kingdom have been cleaned up simply by removing the contamination from one location to another where it has less of an impact. This option has been selected because it is relatively cheap and can be carried out quickly and generally does not delay site development. With increasing landfill disposal costs I doubt whether this option will be available for much longer.

In recent years, in common with other countries (eg the United States, the Netherlands, Germany) the United Kingdom has introduced legislation that not only requires sites to be cleaned up on redevelopment but can, in certain circumstances, provide statutory authorities with the power to clean up sites and recover costs from the landowner. These provisions are contained within the Town and Country Planning Act 1990, the Environmental Protection Act 1990 and the Water Resources Act 1991. Although commonly overlooked, there are also actions in English common law resulting from nuisance and trespass arising from contamination moving from one site to another. These provisions have not been used frequently in the past but I believe an increasing number of legal actions will be taken in the future. Consideration is currently being given in the European Community to the introduction of strict liability for damage to the environment. This, if introduced, could further increase the awareness of those who own or buy and sell property to the liabilities of contaminated land. It could also introduce many more retrospective actions in the courts for environmental damage.

Against this background of increasing awareness of environmental protection, increased costs of waste disposal, the potential liabilities arising from the ownership of land and changing legislation, developers and landowners are taking a much more imaginative and critical look at what they should be doing to rehabilitate land. Financial institutions are also looking very carefully at the liabilities they accept when they lend money for the purchase of land and property. This change in attitudes has resulted in considerable research into the techniques available for the clean-up of contaminated land so that it can be restored to productive use free, as far as practicable, from residual liabilities. The research in clean-up techniques has been led by the United States, the Netherlands and Germany largely as a result of the more prescriptive and retrospective legislation in those countries. The techniques examined in this book include soil washing, bioremediation, incineration and vacuum extraction; the book also reviews some of the emerging technologies in the United States, the Netherlands and Germany. The use of decontamination standards is examined in the context of the high costs of their achievement against the potential benefits of using a risk-based, site-specific assessment approach. Many of the remediation techniques are discussed in the context of actual site work already completed or in research studies currently in progress.

The chapters in this book have been compiled from papers presented at a one-day symposium held by the Institution of Chemical Engineers in London on 31 March 1993. As a result of this there is inevitably some overlap between chapters but this generally serves to reinforce the subject matter.

I commend this book to all those who are looking for a good introduction to existing site remediation techniques and their potential applications.

Malcolm Pratt
Technical Director, Cremer and Warner

Since joining Cremer and Warner, Malcolm Pratt has been involved in a wide range of environmental projects including contaminated land surveys and assessment, development of decontamination criteria and design and implementation of remediation schemes. Other projects have included environmental impact assessments, environmental audits of industrial facilities and presentation of expert evidence at planning inquiries and in the courts.

He has served on the IChemE environmental auditing working party, and has given evidence to a Royal Commission and a select committee of the House of Commons.

THE AUTHORS

1. The role of research, information and demonstration projects
    S.T. Johnson, Research Manager *(Construction Industry Research and Information Association, CIRIA)*

2. North America — current technology and developments
    S. Hughes, Manager Wastewater Department and I. Mugglestone, Manager Waste Management Department *(Brown & Root Environmental)*

3. Soils washing
    C.R. Boyle, Division Manager *(Bergmann Technology)*

4. Biological remediation: a European perspective
    J.H.A.M. Verheul, Project Manager of Environmental Technology, P.J. de Bruijn, Project Director of Environmental Technology *(DHD Netherlands)* and S.M. Herbert, Divisional Director Geotechnical and Environmental Engineering Section *(DHV Burrow-Crocker Consulting UK)*

5. UK current technology and developments
    S. Tillotson, Technical Director *(Environmental Resources Ltd)*

6. *In situ* remediation using vacuum extraction techniques
    G. Licence, Development Manager *(Miller Environmental Ltd)*

7. Mobile incineration
    J. Oesterle, Technical Director, K. McNelis, Chemical Engineer *(Fluor Daniel Inc)* and E.J. McVoy, Incineration Manager *(Contaminant Treatment Inc)*

This book is based on contributions to a symposium organized by the IChemE London and South-Eastern Branch in London on 31 March 1993.

CONTENTS

1. THE ROLE OF RESEARCH, INFORMATION AND DEMONSTRATION PROJECTS

Simon Johnson

While the options available for treatment of contaminated land continue to increase, it is an apparent paradox that the rapid expansion of the knowledge base and the variety of remediation techniques can inhibit, through decision paralysis, their adoption into practice. Research, information and demonstration projects play a central role in supporting and informing both commercial and technical judgements, and in promoting confidence through peer review and wide dissemination.

Over the last few years extensive efforts have been made to recycle contaminated and derelict land in the UK although emphasis has been on derelict land (which may or may not be contaminated). Legislation, and in particular the Environmental Protection Act 1990, the Water Resources Act 1991 and the Planning and Compensation Act 1991 are all relevant to the control of pollution and to the problems posed by contaminated land.

Recycling contaminated and derelict land is a complex operation and will always require specialist input, even more so with the rapid expansion of the range of remediation techniques now available. It is important that developers and their engineering advisers, in making commercial and technical judgements, are confident that they understand both the technology of remediation and changing environmental liabilities. Sharing knowledge and expertise through collaborative research-and-information projects is an effective and economical way of transferring R&D advances into practice. Demonstration projects can further build confidence particularly if subject to review and wide dissemination.

POLICY, LEGISLATION AND ENFORCEMENT

The White Paper in 1990, *This Common Inheritance*[1], commits the present UK government to improving the environment and dealing with serious contamination. Specific to contaminated land are the major policy commitments set out in the government's response[2] to the Environment Committee First Report to the House of Commons[3]. A commitment to support demonstration projects of novel

1

clean-up technologies has recently been confirmed with UK participation in the current phase of the NATO Committee for Challenges to Modern Society (CCMS) Programme on the treatment of contaminated sites.

The European Community Green Paper, EUR12902N, encourages research into contaminated soil clean-up and recommends a programme of pilot projects.

There is a wide range of legislation developed over the last 100 years in the UK relevant to protecting the environment, which now include various EC directives and statutes, and may affect either working on, or transactions involving, contaminated land. In addition to specific legislation and regulations, the wide scope of common law in the UK can provide a remedy for those claiming (or seeking to prevent) actual damage, nuisance and negligence.

Section 143 of the Environmental Protection Act 1990 makes provision for public registers of land which may be contaminated. The Department of the Environment (DoE) has issued, as drafts for consultation, revised guidance for the implementation of the registers. In support, specialists were commissioned to produce typical profiles of the contamination associated with a wide range of industries and site usage.

The Water Resources Act 1991, provides for the National Rivers Authority (NRA) to take action to clean up actual contamination of controlled waters as well as potential pollutants, and to recover the costs. Following consultation, the NRA's policy in controlling the quality of groundwater resources and surface water courses was published in 1992[4]. For new developments, the land-use planning framework acts to protect the Green Belt and safeguard the countryside and to encourage full and effective use of urban land and bringing back into use sites previously developed, including derelict sites.

Urban regeneration is provided for by a number of grant schemes. Arguably the most important of these has been Derelict Land Grants which were introduced in 1966, and the establishment of Development Corporations specifically tasked to bring back into use designated areas of dereliction (eg London Docklands and Trafford Park in Manchester).

In 1976, the DoE established the Interdepartmental Committee on the Redevelopment of Contaminated Land (ICRCL). Between 1976 and 1990, this committee issued a number of guidance notes about the redevelopment of contaminated land. ICRCL 59/83[5], for example, gives trigger levels for a limited range of contaminants.

The recent award of substantial damages (over £1m) against the Eastern

2

Leather Company in favour of the Cambridge Water Company by the Court of Appeal[6] may open the way for more sucessful prosecutions. As a comparison, and perhaps indicative of a general trend, fines for polluters in the USA have risen from $18.5m in 1991 to $49m in the first six months of 1992[7].

THE MARKET

It is estimated that some 50% of all development takes place on previously used land some of which may be contaminated[8]. The UK market for treatment services is thought to be £240m in 1991 rising to £360m by 1993 and over £800m by the year 2000[9]. Similar activity is to be expected in other European countries (Figure 1.1).

Not In My Back Yard (NIMBY) demands will make siting waste disposal facilities more difficult. Fewer acceptable sites, tougher legislative controls, and higher engineering standards being required of landfill operators, will increase the cost for the disposal of contaminated soil (and other materials such as sludges and leachates). Treatment on or off site will become more attractive to developers.

In the USA, a recent report[10] has suggested that the hazardous waste site remediation market will continue to grow from $22bn in 1992 to some $41bn by 1996. Although Environmental Protection Agency (EPA) spending is expected to increase from $2.3bn in 1991 to $6.5bn in 1996, the largest spend is

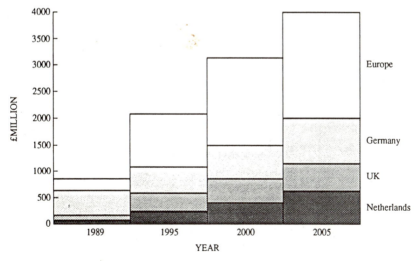

Figure 1.1   Market projections (£m) for remedial treatment services.

3

likely to be on federal facilities up to $23bn in 1996 and in excess of $37bn by 2000. Treatment is likely to favour process-based technologies against a background rise in the cost for disposal to licensed sites of hazardous waste from $10 to $300 a tonne in the last 20 years.

Market projections for the UK and other European countries are very encouraging for companies intending to, or already investing in, remedial technology. However, realization of these figures depends on client confidence to specify technical solutions and a financially active market for treated land. The use of economic instruments, such as taxation or licensing, may also encourage moves away from disposal to landfills.

SALE AND TRANSFER OF CONTAMINATED LAND

Notwithstanding the very real threat of further substantial prosecutions of polluters, the prospect of further devaluation of land values for contaminated sites and liability for treatment is concerning lenders and other stakeholders. This is a particular problem where the land represents the substantial asset and where the lender may become liable for remedial action.

The government's Advisory Committee on Business and the Environment (ACBE) has recently[11] made representation that there should be no fundamental reform of the existing regime of civil liability for environmental damage.

Public pressure is for the best possible environmental protection. Rehabilitating dereliction and treating contamination are seen as positive actions. The public, though wanting improved neighbourhood services and the preservation of green belt and countryside, perceives the remedial treatment of contaminated sites — even within urban regeneration schemes — to have a high risk. The standards of treatment, therefore, have to achieve a viable balance of safety, effectiveness and cost in the short term, and satisfy long-term requirements of reliability, in order to gain wider acceptance.

This situation may be helped by the adoption of widely-accepted procedures in sale and transfer. Some of the many and wide range of issues which need to be considered are listed in Table 1. The Department of the Environment, with joint funding from industry and professional bodies, have commissioned The Construction Industry Research and Information Association (CIRIA) to manage, taking advice from a steering group, the preparation of guideline procedures for the assessment of the impact of contamination on the sale and transfer of land which may be affected by contamination.

TABLE 1.1.

Some of the issues in the sale and transfer of land which may be contaminated

- Legislative framework, including:liability — past, current and future, civil and criminal, strict and tortious; EC Directives and Regulations; and highlight differences between English and Scottish law. Who is an owner? Tenants, residents, lessees, landlords, etc. Planning conditions.

- Condition of the land: what is contamination? How land can become contaminated; how contaminants move and migrate; what are the risks to human health, the environment and to buildings and other structures?

- Site evaluation, what can be found out and at what cost? Principles and rationale for investigation; identification of migratory risks, completeness of information and uncertainties — information which can be obtained and that which is not available because of a genuine gap in knowledge; role of quality assurance/verification in site evaluation; cost/benefit of investigation.

- Status of any information: role and responsibility of the consultant and other experts; responsibilities and liability of the vendor for any information released to the purchaser and recommendations on disclosure of information; role and responsibilities of local authorities.

- Use, role and limitations of published guidelines for clean-up levels for soil and water; effect of background levels of priority contaminants, eg arsenic in the South West.

- Risk assessment, evaluation and management by vendor and purchaser. Use of professional advisors; parallels with other industries, eg chemical manufacturers and insurance; identification of good practice and recommendations.

- Options for treatment and improvement of the site; selection of appropriate measures and the benefit to vendor or purchaser. Operational and post-treatment monitoring and measurement.

- The role and value of insurance, warranties, collateral warranties, duty-of-care, guarantees, etc.

- Valuation, blight and negative asset values. Compulsory purchase and sale.

5

PLANNING REMEDIATION WORKS

The planning process for remedial treatment requires logical progression through a number of stages including consideration of end-use, which will set the initial objectives to guide the choice of remedial method from the options available and procurement of the contractor and other professional services. Depending on the remedial method and on the site to be treated, it may be necessary to draw on available R&D, on reports of similar situations or use of technology, or even to commission specific studies.

When considering or planning to remediate contaminated land, it is becoming necessary:

1. To formulate reclamation strategies which take account of a wide range of policy and regulatory developments.
2. To forecast long-term reliability and impact, and consider future liabilities and obligations.
3. To identify and adopt (and if necessary develop) safe, cost-effective remedial treatment systems and procedures for use on both active and derelict contaminated sites.

In practice, the selection of an appropriate remedial solution is highly site-specific, depending on factors such as those in Figure 1.2.

Many of the issues listed in Figure 1.2 are familiar and common to all construction works, but contamination and its treatment call for additional knowledge, special care and clear objectives. Few organizations are yet likely to have the wide knowledge and experience necessary to compare and assess all

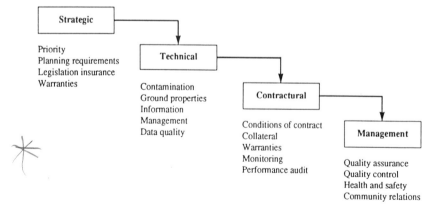

Figure 1.2   Some issues when planning remedial treatment.

the different and possible options for any particular site. It is therefore important to take a holistic risk management approach to analysing and managing the interactions of policy and management issues with technical factors. Good project management provides a suitable and readily understood structure for making these decisions.

In many cases once the contamination problem is identified it is unlikely to present a significant technical challenge. The problem is then to provide a solution which is both environmentally sound, safe, economical and acceptable to all stakeholders.

SETTING OBJECTIVES

The primary objective of any remedial action must be to treat to a standard wherein the risk to specified targets, which will include the environment, is reduced to an acceptable level. In the UK, the concept of functionality prevails, ie the degree of treatment should be appropriate to the end-use. In some instances the end-use may be defined by strategic purpose, thus to treat to a standard whereby potential contingent liabilities are minimized is a legitimate objective.

Functionality provides considerable scope for appropriate remedial treatment and is a philosophy gaining ground in countries which have previously operated multifunctional approaches, where treatment is to a standard set by the most sensitive use — usually housing. Objectives are usually defined by an appropriate level for the contaminants on site and from this information a set of remedial action strategies can be formulated.

Ideally, contaminant-related objectives alone should determine the response made at any particular site. In practice, there may also be engineering or management objectives to be met, such as altering site levels or completion of the works within a defined period, as well as a number of site-specific constraints to be considered. Thus, the cost of the work, the practical difficulties of implementation, the need to reconcile often conflicting objectives and legal or community-based objections to the use of a technically satisfactory solution all have an impact on the selection process.

Such additional objectives and constraints clearly have an important role to play as the evaluation process continues and the definition of appropriate remedial action becomes progressively more refined. Nevertheless, it is important to ensure that the contamination action objectives defined by the site investigation/risk assessment continue to guide the selection process. This avoids the common problem that potentially useful methods are rejected on premature assumptions, and before a reasonably disciplined evaluation of the merits and limitations of alternative methods takes place.

Any strategy aimed at protecting human health and the environment should identify and specify:

- the contaminant(s) of concern and their source;

- exposure route(s) and target(s);

- an acceptable contaminant level, or range of levels, for each exposure route and target.

Treatment methods can reduce the contaminant levels while containment interrupts, or otherwise cuts off, exposure routes. Alternatively, or in combination with treatment or containment the proposed use may be changed (eg from domestic housing to a lorry park and warehouse) to reduce the potential for impact on sensitive targets.

Quantitative objectives are typically expressed in terms of the concentration of contaminants in soils (or other media) which should not be exceeded in the material left on the site following treatment. For example, soils left in place after the excavation of contaminated material, or the reuse of treated material.

Protection of the environment typically aims to preserve or restore a resource (eg groundwater). Environmental objectives, therefore, are usually expressed in terms of the medium of interest and the standard for protection.

Quantitative remedial objectives may be expressed in terms of the quality of the environmental media in contact with a treated site. Other, indirect, quantitative measures may be used to ensure that remedial action objectives are met. For example, a permeability value for a barrier system may be agreed in order to ensure that the concentrations of contaminants in groundwater in contact with the barrier system do not exceed specified drinking water standards or other specific quality objectives.

OPTIONS FOR REMEDIAL TREATMENT

Disposal to licensed landfill, cap and cover, or containment are likely to remain, at least in the near future, a first choice remedial solution in the UK. Disposal has a number of advantages over technology based treatment processes, including:

- a comparatively low cost, which can be estimated relatively easily;

- client confidence in a proven solution;

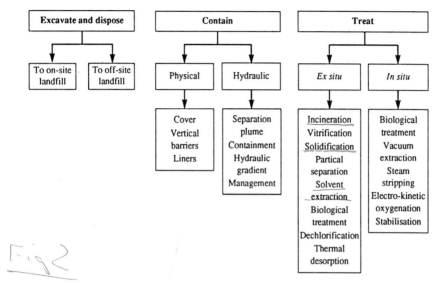

Figure 1.3   Categories of treatment.

• the appearance of removing the contamination from the development site;

• low technology — easily understood.

But licensing, duty-of-care obligations and NIMBY concerns are driving up the cost of landfill and closing the economic gap with alternative solutions. The range of remediation options which can be considered is categorized in Figure 1.3.

Obviously different methods apply to the various contaminants and whether soils or groundwater are to be treated.

Defining the areas or volumes needing to be treated requires consideration of:

• acceptable exposure levels and potential routes;

• site conditions;

• nature and extent of contamination.

For example, where contaminants are homogeneously distributed in a medium, discrete risk levels (eg 1 in 100,000 cancer risk) or corresponding contaminant concentrations, may provide the most rational basis for defining areas or volumes to be treated. Conversely, where discrete hot spots or areas of severe contamination are present, it may be more useful to define areas or volumes of media on a unit area basis.

Options does not necessarily mean the choice between a number of rigidly defined methods, rather it invites a systems approach to the problem. Recent work at Warren Spring Laboratory in the UK emphasizes the advantages of using well-proven minerals processing techniques to initially fractionate the soil. A single site can often present a number of different contamination problems both in the type of contaminant and how the contamination is associated with the particular soil fraction, eg adhered or absorbed. Preprocessing and fractionation can significantly reduce the volumes of materials requiring treatment or disposal.

SELECTION OF REMEDIAL TREATMENT

A formal selection process enables a full range of options to be considered and compared within a logical framework for assessing cost, performance, safety, regulatory compliance, resource requirements, etc. Stages and tasks described may overlap considerably, or even be omitted, depending on the size and complexity of the site, and the magnitude of the risks involved. The important point is that all options are considered equally, within recognized and site-specific constraints.

Documenting the process aids justification and the communication of ideas, results and decisions to all relevant parties.

The process, once the remedial action objectives have been set and site-specific constraints identified, consists of:

• identifying general response actions (eg non-technical measures, removal, containment, clean-up) which taken singly, or in combination, meet the requirements of the remedial action objectives;

• determining volumes or areas of contaminated media to which general response actions can be applied;

• identifying methods, and associated process options, appropriate to each general response action identified; and the elimination of methods which, for technical reasons, are not capable of practical implementation at the site;

• assembling selected methods into a range of alternative remedial strategies for the treatment of the site as a whole;

• further screening of alternative remedial strategies where necessary.

Depending on circumstances, alternative remedial strategies may be developed for the site as a whole, individual areas of a site (eg lagoon, waste stockpile), or for a specific medium (eg groundwater). The selection process may be carried through as a series of separate exercises, or combined at some earlier point to provide a comprehensive strategy for the entire site. Addressing key elements in the selection process, illustrated in Figure 1.4, allows for a progressively more refined definition of potential remedial alternatives strategies.

CONTRACTS AND SPECIFICATIONS

Traditionally standard civil engineering or building conditions of contract have been used: Institution of Civil Engineers (5th), Institution of Chemical Engineers and Department of Transport conditions (where the project involves major road building) are all examples. However, it is clear that remedial treatment — and in particular the phased and iterative process of site evaluation, investigation and assessment — may require more flexible arrangements, or at least fully exploit the inherent flexibility in most conditions of contract.

To work best, any contract needs trust and positive client/advisor/contractor relations. The degree of uncertainty and outcome in some treatment situations is reflected in the recent decision by the US Navy[12] to award in early 1993 a number of cost-plus indefinite-delivery contracts of between $40m and $60m each for five years on one year renewals.

Specifying the work requires equal care and recognition of the problem. The principle is that the specification should relate to the levels of contamination

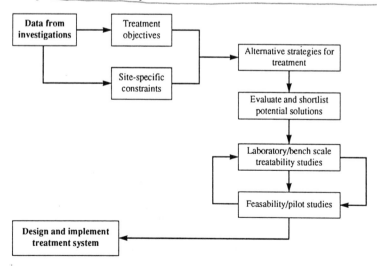

Figure 1.4   Key elements in the selection process.

11

TABLE 1.2

Analysis of papers presented at 2nd HMCRI National R&D Conference, February 1992

Subject	% papers	
R&D	36	
R&I and management	16	
Applications	23	
Site assessment	21	
Safety	4	

Technology		EPA take-up (12)
Physical	6	12
Chemical	15	8
Biological	27	15
Vapour extraction	38	27
Incineration/thermal	6	38
Pump-and-treat	13	n/a

and more particularly to each of the source, pathway, target elements. It is necessary to be clear on what is to be achieved, how it will be achieved and with what degree of certainty, operational life, etc. While difficult, by taking this approach, combined with good project management, no action will be taken without purpose or understanding.

R&D, DEMONSTRATIONS AND COLLABORATIVE PROJECTS

At the second US National R&D conference, run by the Hazardous Materials Control Resources Institute (HMCRI), an appreciation of the papers (Table 1.2) gave the following approximate breakdown based on common categories for subject matter and treatment technology. Many were R&D reports and prior to any formal demonstration of the technology, even at pilot scale.

Comparison with the latest EPA summary of the take-up of innovative and established treatment technologies for control of contaminant sources at Superfund sites[13], in particular, highlights the current use of thermal treatment, which is considered to be relatively well proven. Many of the innovative technologies are mostly at pilot and demonstration stages.

There are a number of common themes and objectives for R&D

irrespective of country of origin:

• improved remediation techniques are required to achieve significantly faster (than at present) and economical treatment;

• greater confidence is needed in site characterization and site sampling strategies;

• more effective *in situ* treatment methods should be developed as a long-term goal;

• qualified, multi-disciplinary regulators are needed to encourage innovative approaches to remediation;

• support should be given for centres of excellence for R&D. Co-ordination of effort will avoid unnecessary overlap and promote a consistent and technically rigorous approach to R&D;

• communication and early dissemination of research and demonstration results in a form, and with an independence, which encourages the confidence of the industry and its clients.

For some 30 years, CIRIA has addressed this last point by carrying out and widely disseminating the results of research and information projects. The projects undertaken are relevant, timely and needed by the members of the association and the wider industry. For each project, a balanced steering group of experts, and other interested professionals provides guidance on the scope, technical sufficiency and objectivity.

By careful selection of the contractor, and with the wide-ranging input of the steering group, the work is recognized by all sides of industry as independent and authoritative. An important aspect is the way the project is funded by contributions both from government and different industry interests. DoE, as the sponsor department for construction research, has long given major support to CIRIA projects in general and recently to the Geo-environmental programme on contaminated sites and their hazards, Figure 1.5 overleaf.

The first phase of this programme concentrated on bringing together the vast pool of knowledge and information on all stages in the remedial treatment of contaminated sites in the form of a handbook which is applicable to the client and non-specialist engineer[17]. Phase II is designed to provide state-of-the-art reviews and detailed guidance on those techniques used, primarily, for containment and control against contaminant migration.

The third phase of the programme extends the state-of-the-art reviews and guidance to *in situ* and *ex situ* treatment methods and systems. It further

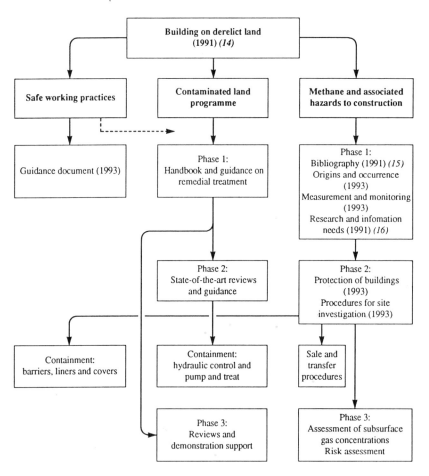

Figure 1.5   CIRIA geo-environmental programme.

proposes to manage and disseminate information from one or more collaborative projects demonstrating good practice procedures on site and in the laboratory for the assessment and selection of appropriate treatment and of treatment processes or systems which are relatively new (at least in their application in the UK).

This proposal is particularly timely, for there is an increase in interest and activity in the application of treatment technologies and the full participation of the government in the next phase of the NATO Committee for Challenges to

Modern Society (CCMS) initiative on contaminated land. The NATO CCMS programme presents a unique opportunity to share experience through dissemination of information on technology demonstrations and applications.

Close liaison with the relevant government departments ensures that there is a minimum of unnecessary repetition and maximum synergy of effort. The current programme at CIRIA complements other research and information work sponsored by the DoE on identifying, assessing and dealing with contamination[18].

In addition there are a number of other initiatives and research efforts supported by the government either directly or through the research grants system.

CONCLUSIONS

It is important that remediation of contaminated land is treated as a logical process, adopting the usual project management, risk management and planning disciplines associated with general construction and other process engineering works. The selection procedure needs to be planned with sufficient flexibility and contingency for a phased approach incorporating the elements of investigation, assessment, initial selection, treatability and feasibility studies, final selection and planning for implementing the chosen solution.

Information programmes like CIRIA's, if they are to be up to date, have to tap into the work of other organizations actively dealing with or researching contaminated land issues and complement other public funded research and information programmes. The benefit is two-fold and mutual: better advice is given to practitioners; and there is wider, perhaps more rapid, and certainly effective dissemination of the findings of the other organizations. In a matter of such importance to a country's health and well-being, the sooner knowledge is put into practice the better.

From work over the last few years to provide guidance and information on the treatment of derelict and contaminated sites CIRIA has noted that:

1. The various persons and organizations involved in contaminated-land engineering want different types of information in order to be confident of applying R&D advances into practice.
2. Cross-disciplinary, multi-sponsor, collaborative projects are an effective and economical way to provide that information and to highlight uncertainties.
3. Statements of soundly based, good practice, which show the interactions between policy, legislation, development, viability and standards are the key

step between R&D and the appropriate application of technology.

4. The willingness of specialists, industry and government to contribute to projects of the type being carried out by CIRIA not only confirms the suitability of this approach to technology transfer, but also emphasizes the urgent need for it.

REFERENCES

1. *This Common Inheritance: Britain's Environmental Strategies, CM 1200*, 1990, HMSO, London.
2. *CM 1161, Contaminated Land*, 1990, HMSO, London.
3. *Environment Committee, First Report, Contaminated Land*, 1990, HMSO, London.
4. Anon, *Policy and Practice for the Protection of Groundwater*, National Rivers Authority, December 1992
5. ICRCL (Interdepartmental committee on the redevelopment of contaminated land), *Circular 59/83, Guidance on assessment and redevelopment of contaminated land*, 2nd Ed. May 1983, Department of the Environment, Central Directorate on Environmental Pollution, London.
6. *Financial Times*, 25 November 1992.
7. *HMCRI Focus*, Volume 8, No.10, Hazardous Materials Control Resources Institute, USA, November 1992.
8. Petts, J. Contaminated land, overview of current issues and concerns, *Proc Conf on Contaminated Land: Policy, regulation and technology*, Conference Document E7568, IBC, London, 1991.
9. Haines, R.C., Scale and extent of contaminated land in the UK — an opportunity for the construction industry?, *Proc Conf on Contaminated Land, A practical examination of the technical and legal issues*, Conference Document E7588, IBC, London, 1991.
10. *HMCRI Focus*, Volume 8, No.11, Hazardous Materials Control Resources Institute, USA, December 1992
11. *ENDS Report No.214*, Environmental Data Services Ltd. London, November 1992.
12. *ENR Volume 229*, No.22, McGraw-Hill, USA, November 1992.
13. *Vendor Information System for Innovative Treatment Technologies (VISITT)*, United States Environmental Protection Agency, EPA/542/N-92/002, No.1 June 1992.
14. Leach, B.A. and Goodger, H.K., *Building on derelict land, Special Publication 78*, CIRIA, London, 1991.
15. Hartless, R. (Compiler), *Methane and associated hazards to construction — a bibliography, Special Publication 79*, CIRIA, London, 1991.
16. Wardell Armstrong, *Methane and associated hazards to construction — research and information needs, Project Report 5*, CIRIA, London, 1991.
17. Johnson, S.T., Smith, M.A., Harris, M.R. and Herbert, S.M., Guidance for construc-

tion on contaminated sites, *Fourth International KfK/TNO Conf on Contaminated Soil, Berlin, May 1993* (to be published).

18. Department of the Environment, *DoE Research Market: 1991, Newsletter*, Chief Scientist Group

ACKNOWLEDGEMENTS

This paper is published by permission of the Director General of CIRIA and the Department of the Environment. The views expressed are those of the author.

2. NORTH AMERICA — CURRENT TECHNOLOGY AND DEVELOPMENT

Ian Mugglestone and Stephen Hughes

North American contaminated land remediation technologies have developed, for the most part, in response to the US federal regulations that address the clean-up of abandoned hazardous waste sites, and with the assistance of the US Environmental Protection Agency Superfund Innovative Technology Evaluation (SITE) programme. The broad spectrum of remediation technologies that have been developed can be categorized as physical, chemical, thermal, biological and solidification/stabilization processes. Selected representative technologies from these process categories are presented and briefly described. Finally, a brief overview of emerging remediation technologies is provided.

GOVERNMENT ACTION

The origins of contaminated land remediation technology industry in North America as it exists today can be traced principally to the passage of the Comprehensive Environmental Response, Compensation and Liability Act (CERCLA) by the US Federal Government in 1980. Before CERCLA was enacted there were no specific laws in place that addressed the environmental problems created by abandoned hazardous waste sites. A series of nationally publicized environmental incidents in the late 1970s, such as Love Canal in New York and Valley of the Drums in Kentucky, led to strong public pressure on government to pass legislation to enable the remediation of abandoned environmentally hazardous sites where the owners and/or responsible parties could not, for a variety of reasons, initiate or complete a proper environmentally acceptable clean-up.

An integral part of CERCLA was the establishment of a $1.6bn 'Superfund' that was to be used over a five year period to, among other things, identify abandoned hazardous waste sites, define the types and extent of hazardous materials present, determine the risk those materials posed to human health and the environment, and remediate the sites to reduce the risks to acceptable levels. CERCLA was re-authorized in 1986 as the Superfund Amendments and Reauthorization Act (SARA), which strengthened some of the original CER-

CLA statutes and appropriated an additional $8.5bn to the programme. The criteria used by the USEPA to determine the required clean-up standards and applicable remediation technologies for Superfund sites and other hazardous waste sites are based generally on the assessed environmental risks at each specific site. Regulations discourage the use of containment methods that attempt to isolate the contaminants on site in an untreated state. Off-site disposal of the contaminated material is also discouraged and is becoming increasingly prohibited by ever-increasing landfill charges and restrictions. Emphasis is therefore placed on remediating hazardous materials so that they pose no present or future risk to human health and the environment.

Contaminated land sites can often contain a wide variety of contaminant types, and therefore can require a wide array of remediation approaches to satisfy the clean-up standards set for the various contaminant species.

In order to progress the state-of-the-art in contaminated land remediation technologies, the USEPA set up the SITE programme in 1985. Under this programme:

'EPA enters into cooperative agreements with innovative technology developers. Through these collaborative efforts, innovative technologies are refined at bench- and pilot-scale and demonstrated at hazardous waste sites. EPA collects and evaluates extensive performance and cost data on each technology, which can aid in future decision-making for hazardous waste remediation'.

Many of the contaminated land remediation technologies presently being used in North America are participants or graduates of the SITE programme. They include a broad spectrum of processes from thermal treatment such as incineration, chemical systems such as solvent extraction and UV oxidation, biological systems such as bioventing, physical systems such as soil washing and vacuum extraction, and solidification/stabilization methods. In the following sections a representative technology from this selected cross-section of processes will be presented and briefly described, with the exception of the soil washing and vacuum extraction technologies which are presented in further detail elsewhere in this book (see pages 33 and 113).

We conclude with brief descriptions of some of the more promising newer remediation technologies currently being evaluated in the SITE Programme.

INCINERATION

Incineration has long been recognized as an applicable *ex situ* technology for removing toxic organics from contaminated soils and substances. Incineration processes can be divided into two main categories:

• two stage systems that use volatilization and/or pyrolysis to convert the toxic compounds into the gaseous phase, and then thermal combustion or condensation of the gaseous organics;

• one stage systems that destroy the toxic organics directly within the contaminated soil or substance. End products of incineration are bottom ash, which is normally returned to the original site for backfilling or discharged to landfill, and gaseous emissions which usually undergo treatment to remove fly ash, residual organics and acidic gases.

An example of effective mobile incineration technology is an infrared thermal destruction unit (TDU) that is owned and operated by OHM Remediation Services Corporation (see Figure 2.1). The contaminated material to be treated is fed into the TDU from the feed hopper by a weigh-belt conveyor, where the feed rate is continuously monitored and recorded. The contaminated material is then discharged on to a conveyor belt in the primary chamber and exposed to infrared radiation from silicon carbide rods located above the belt. As the contaminated material travels on the belt through the chamber, it is exposed to the thermal conditions necessary for the volatilization, pyrolysis and/or thermal

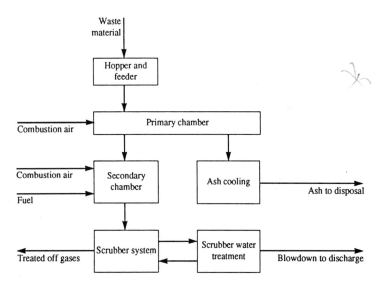

Figure 2.1   OHM infrared thermal destruction.

destruction of the toxic organics. Combustion air is blown into the primary chamber to promote organics combustion, thus providing an additional supply of heat.

Off gases from the primary chamber are drawn into the secondary chamber where residual gaseous organics undergo further thermal destruction at a higher temperature. The treated off gas stream finally enters a scrubber system to remove acidic gases, sulphur dioxide and particulate matter before emission to atmosphere. Recirculating water from the scrubber is clarified and pH adjusted and returned to the scrubber. A blowdown stream undergoes further treatment before discharging to an approved sewer or surface water.

Ash discharged from the primary chamber is indirectly cooled in a screw conveyor, sprayed with water to effect additional cooling and to control fugitive dust emission, and finally discharged by a bucket conveyor to a disposal collection area.

To date, the OHM infrared thermal destruction unit has been used to remediate PCB-contaminated soils at two USEPA Superfund sites and one site for the Canadian Department of National Defence.

One Superfund site in Florida had fill material and sediments contaminated with PCB concentrations as high as 13,900 mg/kg. Using the OHM thermal destruction unit, the PCB concentration in the soil and sediment was reduced to 2 mg/kg and treated off gas emissions demonstrated a PCB destruction and removal efficiency of 99.9999%.

SOLVENT EXTRACTION

Solvent extraction processes have to be shown to be effective in treating soils, sediments and oily sludges contaminated with a wide range of toxic organics including herbicides, pesticides, polynuclear aromatic hydrocarbons (PAHs) and polychlorinated biphenyls (PCBs). The treatment, which normally takes place *ex situ*, typically involves the addition of an extracting solvent to separate the organic contaminants from the solids and water fractions of the contaminated soils and sludges. The separated organics fraction can then be recovered for reuse or incinerated, the water fraction usually undergoes further treatment before final discharge, and the solids fraction is normally returned to the original site for backfilling.

A good example of mobile solvent extraction technology is the BEST (Basic Extraction Sludge Treatment) process, developed by the Resources Conservation Company, which uses triethylamine (TEA) as the extracting solvent (see Figure 2.2). The contaminated soil or waste to be treated is mixed with cold TEA to create a suspension of solids within a homogeneous, single-phase liquid containing solvent, water and organic contaminants, and the pH is adjusted to alkaline to avoid protonation of the TEA. Due to its inverse misci-bility properties, TEA is mutually soluble with water at temperatures below 20°C. This allows intimate contact with solutes at nearly ambient temperatures and pressures, and permits high extraction efficiencies to be maintained during the treatment of feed mixtures with high water and/or oil content.

Once the extraction process has been completed, the solids are removed from the mixture by gravity settling and/or centrifugation, and dried to recover residual TEA. The remaining TEA/water/organic contaminant mixture is then separated into its components. The organic fraction is concentrated by evapora-ting and condensing the solvent/water mixture. After condensing, the tempera-ture of the solvent/water mixture is above the miscible range and the solvent and water phases are easily separated by decantation since there is a significant difference in the densities of each. The traces of residual TEA remaining in the water and organic contaminant phases are removed by steam stripping. The recovered TEA is reused in subsequent extraction cycles.

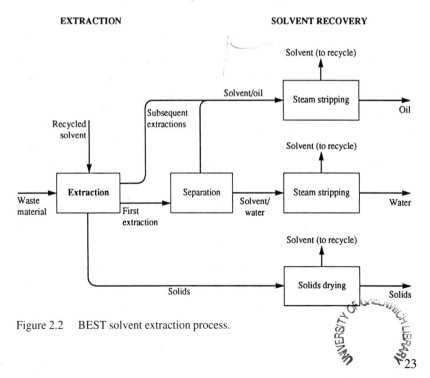

Figure 2.2   BEST solvent extraction process.

To date the BEST process has been used at ten sites in the USA to treat a variety of contaminated soils, sludges and sediments generated by petroleum refining, coke and steel manufacturing, aluminium manufacturing and wood treating operations, among others. PCB concentrations ranging from 5 to 800 mg/kg have been reduced to 1.0 mg/kg or less. PAH concentrations were typically reduced by greater than 99%. The BEST process has been selected by the USEPA for the remediation of a Superfund site contaminated with PCBs and PAHs under the SITE programme.

SOLIDIFICATION/STABILIZATION
Solidification/stabilization processes have been used to convert contaminated liquids, sludges and soils into a chemically and physically stable solid material with the addition of binding agents. The binding agents are typically inorganic materials such as cement, fly ash, pozzolans and silicates, although organic materials such as asphalt, epoxy resins and polyesters have been used. The goal of a solidification/stabilization process is to reduce the toxicity and mobility of the toxic contaminants by binding them into a tightly-formed solid matrix that resists degradation and leaching.

A good example of an inorganic solidification/stabilization technology is the Chemfix process developed by Chemfix Technologies, Inc (see Figure 2.3). The contaminated material to be treated is fed into a series of blending and mixing reactors where silica, calcium and alumina reagents are added and dissolved in the liquid phase. Water may have to be added to the mix if sufficient moisture is not present within the waste material to promote the required chemical reactions. Metallic contaminants react with the reagents to form inorganic polymers, which bind any organic colloided material into the polymer matrix. The silicates then react with complex ions in the presence of a setting agent to form a silicate gel and precipitating agent. Most of the heavy metal precipitates are chemically bound within the silicate gel matrix. Those heavy metal precipitates that are not chemically bound are physically caught within the silicate gel structure and immobilized.

If organic contaminants are entrained within particles that are not physically bound by the silicate gel matrix, they are emulsified by the mechanical action of the blending equipment and the addition of surfactants. The emulsified organics are microencapsulated and solidified as the silicate gel sets up and hardens.

To date, the Chemfix technology has been used at over ten sites in the

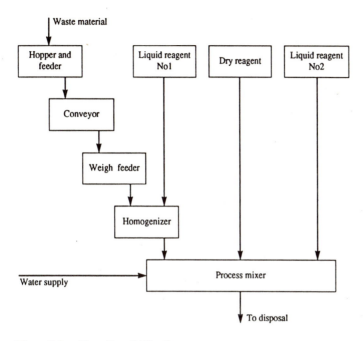

Figure 2.3   Chemfix solidification process.

USA to solidify contaminated materials from steel manufacturing and metal finishing facilities, chemical plants, petroleum refineries and hazardous waste landfills, among others. The contaminated materials included chrome-contaminated flue dust, refinery and heavy metal sludges, electroplating wastes, industrial wastes containing chlorinated hydrocarbons and low level radioactive slag.

At one hazardous waste landfill site, sludge generated from leachate treatment was treated by the Chemfix process and the leachability for most heavy metals and organics was reduced by over 99%. At another waste site, arsenic and hydrofluoric acids were reduced to a non-hazardous solid with a volume increase of less than 150%.

BIOVENTING
A relatively new, but effective, biological method for removing volatile and semivolatile organics from soil and groundwater *in situ* is a technology category recently given the name of bioventing. As with many *in situ* volatilization methods, bioventing uses the combination of *in situ* soil vapour extraction and air stripping (sparging) to create an air flow pattern through the contaminated

25

soil and groundwater. The bioventing system, however, is designed and operated in such a matter that biological degradation becomes the main organics removal process, and not volatilization. Bioventing requires little or no vented off gas treatment, and no *ex situ* groundwater treatment.

A good example of bioventing technology is the Sub-surface Volatilization and Ventilation System (SVVS) developed by Billings and Associates, Inc. Before SVVS is installed, the phase-separated free product layer that normally floats above the groundwater water table is typically reduced or eliminated. This is accomplished by the use of product recovery filters (PRF) which consist of cylindrical hydrophobic membranes that are installed in boreholes positioned within the free product plume. As the free product passes through the hydrophobic membrane, it collects in a reservoir connected to the bottom of the filter and is periodically pumped to the surface. Typically, the free product recovered contains less than 5% water and can usually be shipped directly to a recycling facility.

After free product recovery has been accomplished, SVVS is installed (see Figure 2.4). The system consists of a series of reactor nests positioned within the contaminated soil and groundwater, interconnecting piping and air delivery and vacuum units. Each reactor nest consists of an air injection line located below the groundwater table in the saturated zone and an air extraction line located in the vadose zone above the groundwater table and capillary fringe. As air is sparged into the saturated zone from the air injection line, it strips volatile and semivolatile organics from the groundwater and saturated soil. After the air/organics bubbles have migrated to the surface of the groundwater table, they are drawn to the air extraction line by negative pressure. As the organics pass through the oxygen enriched and moisture-laden vadose zone, indigenous microbes absorb the organics and biodegrade them.

The rate at which air can be sparged and extracted can be modulated at each reactor nest by valve adjustment, thus allowing the bioremediation process to be controlled and optimized. As the indigenous microbial population increases and more organics are absorbed and digested, the organic concentration in the vented vacuum-extracted off gas decreases and off gas treatment is often not required after the initial start-up phase.

To date, SVVS has been successfully used to clean up approximately sixty petrol station sites in a variety of soil conditions. Groundwaters have been typically remediated to drinking water quality, and water quality has been maintained after SVVS has been removed. SVVS recently was selected to remediate a Superfund site contaminated with chlorinated hydrocarbons under the USEPA SITE programme.

UV OXIDATION

Ultraviolet (UV) oxidation technology has been successfully used to destroy soluble organics in contaminated groundwaters. The treatment occurs *ex situ* after the groundwater has been pumped to the surface. Some of the contaminants treated by UV/oxidation include petrol components, solvents, pesticides, explosives and wood preserving chemicals. It is particularly effective on toxic organic compounds, such as chlorinated hydrocarbons, that are resistant to biological degradation. The process oxidizes the toxic organics by rapid chemical and photochemical reactions, and converts them into carbon dioxide, water, salts and harmless organic acids.

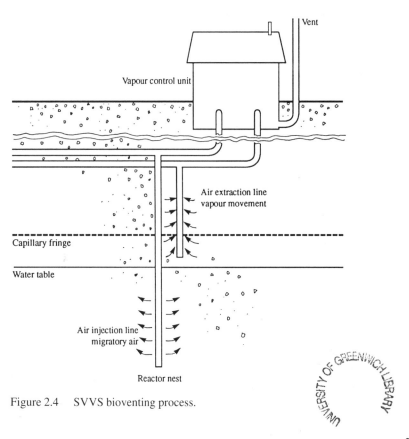

Figure 2.4   SVVS bioventing process.

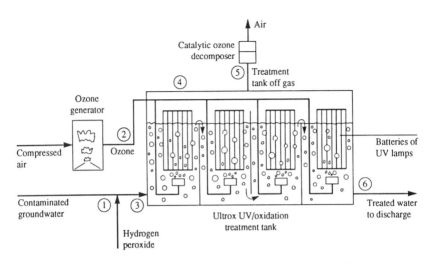

Figure 2.5   Ultrox/UV oxidation process. 1   Hydrogen peroxide is combined with contaminated water; 2   Ozone is generated and injected into the treatment tank; 3   Contaminated water is pumped to the treatment tank and irradiated with ultraviolet light. The light reacts with the ozone gas and hydrogen peroxide, producing hydroxyl radicals which destroy organic contaminants; 4   Water flows from left to right through a series of treatment chambers; 5   Residual ozone in the off gas is converted to oxygen by a catalytic decomposer, eliminating any release of ozone; 6   Treated water flows to discharge.

Chemically, UV/oxidation is achieved through the direct action of ozone and/or hydrogen peroxide and the highly reactive hydroxyl radical, which is created from the reaction of UV light with ozone and/or hydrogen peroxide. The hydroxyl radical is an unstable entity containing of hydrogen and oxygen atoms with 2.05 times the oxidation power of chlorine, 1.58 times the oxidation power of hydrogen peroxide and 1.35 times the oxidation power of ozone. Photochemically, UV light acts directly to break the bonds of organic molecules and indirectly by creating more hydroxyl radicals. The UV/oxidant combination reacts far more quickly and effectively to oxidize organic compounds than either UV light or any oxidant acting alone.

A good example of UV/oxidation technology is the Ultrox System, which uses both ozone and hydrogen peroxide in combination with UV light (see Figure 2.5). Hydrogen peroxide is added to the contaminated groundwater before it is pumped to the treatment tank, where the UV/oxidation reaction takes place. Ozone generated from an air or pure oxygen source is injected into the treatment tank and bubbled up through the contaminated groundwater/hydrogen peroxide mixture. UV light from lamps located in the treatment tank reacts with the ozone and hydrogen peroxide to produce hydroxyl radicals. Organic contaminants react with the oxidants and UV light, and are destroyed. The off gas from the ozone feed stream is passed through a catalytic decomposer at the top of the treatment tank to eliminate the possibility of releasing ozone to the atmosphere.

The Ultrox UV/oxidation system has been used at seven sites in the USA to treat groundwater contaminated with toluene, PCE, TCE, phenols, benzene, ethylbenzene, xylenes, complexed cyanides and various other chlorinated solvents. Initial contaminant concentrations ranged as high as 600 ppb and were in most cases reduced by 99+%. In one instance the treated water was used as a drinking water supply. The Ultrox process was used at a Superfund site to treat groundwater contaminated with chlorinated solvents under the USEPA SITE Programme.

EMERGING TECHNOLOGIES
Within the USEPA SITE programme there exists a subset programme called Emerging Technologies, which is used to develop promising remediation technologies that are in the conceptual stages of development. A representative sample of some of these technologies is presented on this section.

FUNGAL TREATMENT TECHNOLOGY
Developed by the USEPA Risk Reduction Engineering Laboratory and the USDA Forest Products Laboratory, this process uses white rot fungi to remediate soils *in situ*. Woodchips and fungi are mechanically blended into the soil, and as the fungi biodegrades the wood, it also digests the organic contaminants in the soil. The process has been shown to be effective in soils contaminated with wood-preserving chemicals, PAHs and chlorinated organics.

IN SITU ELECTROACOUSTIC SOIL DECONTAMINATION
Developed by Battelle Memorial Institute, this technology uses electrical and acoustic fields to remove inorganic contaminants from contaminated clayey soils. A direct current electrical field is set up between anodes and cathodes placed in the contaminated soil. The cations in the wet soil migrate towards the cathodes, thus accelerating the precipitation of heavy metal contaminants. An

acoustic field is set up in the middle of the electrical field to help keep interstitial pores within the soil matrix from clogging.

CCBA PHYSICAL AND CHEMICAL TREATMENT
This *ex situ* technology, developed by the Western Product Recovery Group, Inc, converts heavy metal contaminants in sludges, soils and sediments to non-leaching silicates, and oxidizes organic contaminants and binds the residual ash into a ceramic pellet matrix. The process uses clays with specific ion exchange properties to achieve the required physical and chemical bonding of the heavy metals. The resultant ceramic pellet formed in the process can be backfilled at the original site or used as a construction material aggregate.

PHOTOLYTIC AND BIOLOGICAL SOIL DETOXIFICATION
Developed by the IT Corporation, this *in situ* process is a two step system that uses photolytic and biological processes to remediate soils contaminated with organics at shallow depths. Initially the soil is tilled and surfactants added to mobilize the organics. UV lights are then placed over the tilled soil to react with the organics and convert them into compounds that can be more easily biodegraded. Bioremediation is then initiated by the addition of microorganisms, nutrients and additional soil tilling.

X-RAY TREATMENT
This *ex situ* technology, developed by Pulse Sciences, Inc, uses X-rays to remediate soils and sludges contaminated with volatile and semivolatile organics. The ionizing radiation creates a shower of energetic secondary electrons within the contaminated material. The electrons break up the complex organic molecules and form highly reactive radicals that initiate secondary reactions which result in end products of water, carbon dioxide and oxygen.

BIBLIOGRAPHY
1. USEPA, 1991, *The Superfund Innovative Technology Evaluation Program: Technology Profiles*, Fourth Edition, EPA/540/5-91/008, USEPA, Office of Solid Waste and Emergency Response.
2. Armishaw, R., Bardos, R.P., Dunn, R.M., Hill, J.M., Pearl, M., Rampling, T. and Wood, P.A., 1992, *Review of Innovative Contaminated Soil Clean-up Processes, Report LR 819(MR)*, Warren Spring Laboratory.
3. Cairney, T. (Ed.), 1993, *Contaminated Land Problems and Solutions*, Blackie Academic and Professional.

4. Hay, G.H., McCartney, G.J., 1991, Mobile Infrared Incineration of PCB-Contaminated Soils, in *Remediation*, Executive Enterprises Publication.
5. Resources Conservation Company, 1988, Hazardous Waste Cleanup Brochure.
6. Ludlum, R., 1993, Resources Conservation Company, personal communication.
7. Pizzitola, S., 1993, Chemfix Environmental Services, Inc, personal communication.
8. Ardito, C.R. and Billings, J.F., 1991, Alternative Remediation Strategies: The Subsurface Volatilization and Ventilation System, *NWWA/API Conference on Petroleum Hydrocarbons and Organic Chemicals in Groundwater, Houston, USA*.
9. Ultrox, 1992, *The Ultrox UV/Oxidation Process: On-Site Destruction of Organics in Water*, Technical Booklet.

3. SOILS WASHING

Clive Boyle

Volume reduction by soils washing is emerging as one of the most versatile and cost effective methods of dealing with contaminated land or dredged sediments. This chapter describes the principles of soils washing and, by reference to specific case studies, demonstrates how its application can substantially reduce overall treatment or off-site disposal costs.

Treatment or removal of contamination is fundamental to the redevelopment of former industrial land. Further, increasing legislative and environmental pressures are being applied to landowners or users of land in the UK. Greater public awareness, the proposed Section 143 Registers and the awakening of the financial and insurance institutions to this issue will ensure that contaminated land investigations and reclamation will remain important activities for many years to come.

In the UK the most commonly employed methods for dealing with contaminated land fall into the 'conventional engineering' category[1] (eg on-site containment or excavation and removal to landfill). Arguably these methods delay or transfer a potential threat of further contamination for someone else at another time and place, rather than solving it permanently. Changing environmental constraints and the associated rising costs of these conventional methods mean that on-site treatment of contamination is becoming increasingly attractive.

While various on-site treatment methods have been widely employed elsewhere in Europe and in North America for some years, their use in UK has to date been quite limited. Considering specifically those techniques which require initial excavation of the contaminated material (*ex situ*) a small number of projects have been completed using various chemical, biological or thermal treatment processes. Some of these processes are well proven and widely practised elsewhere; others fall into the innovative or development categories. Some good results have been obtained. However, two factors have limited the more widespread adoption of these clean-up technologies:

- Many processes are very contaminant specific and work well when faced with a single contaminant or family of contaminants. On most real sites — particu-

33

larly where former industrial use has been mixed — the contamination will also be mixed, with a broad spectrum of contaminant types and a variable pattern of contamination across the site.

• The more important block to the widespread use of proven and available *ex situ* treatment techniques is an economic one. Assuming that money is available for cleaning up the site from the landowner, user or developer, with or without grants or funding, then the lowest cost solution will understandably be selected in most cases. To date this has led to the majority of sites being dealt with by conventional engineering methods.

There is no doubt that properly-controlled landfill and engineered containment have an important role to play in dealing with the legacy of contaminated land in the UK. There is, however, an understandable reaction against transportation of large volumes of contaminated material by road for redeposition elsewhere, or retention of large volumes of such material on a site being redeveloped for housing or public amenity use. It is widely held to be desirable to minimize the use of these disposal routes by adopting at least some degree of on-site treatment. However, economics will inevitably prevail. If on-site treatment is to be adopted then it must be seen to be not only technically feasible, safe and effective, but also cost effective when compared with landfill or containment.

One technology which is emerging as a widely applicable and versatile tool for minimizing the volume of material for off-site disposal or containment, or for improving the cost-effectiveness of other specialized treatment technologies, is soils washing.

Soils washing has been used extensively elsewhere in Europe[2] (principally Holland, Belgium and Germany) since the early 1980s. More recently the technology has been used in North America. There have been few examples to date on UK sites and the time would now appear to be right for its more widespread adoption.

Bergmann, part of the British group Harrisons and Crosfield plc, has been a major provider of soils washing plant in Europe and North America, and in the past 18 months has turned its attention to the UK, carrying out feasibility studies and developing projects for the use of soils washing in this country.

Soils washing is a technique firmly based upon classical mineral processing and water/wastewater treatment techniques. These techniques have been adapted by specialist companies such as Bergmann over the past ten years for effective use in contaminated land reclamation. Soils washing, therefore, does not fall into the category of developing or unproven technologies. It is available, widely used and reliable (the equipment used being robust and easily operated, reflecting its origins in the minerals and processing industry).

Secondly, while the main thrust of this book is at contaminated land, soils washing is as applicable — and in many cases very cost effective — when used to process dredged sediments from rivers, canals, docks or harbours. This point will be illustrated later in the chapter, and further references to soil should be taken to encompass dredged sediments as well.

What I aim to do is explain the underlying principles of soils washing and describe the main 'typical' process steps. Specific examples then show how soils washing can be used, and demonstrate that the technology can meet the two criteria of technical acceptability and cost-effectiveness.

PRINCIPLES OF SOILS WASHING

Soils washing is a term applied to a number of treatment processes for use on contaminated land sites including *in situ* and organic solvent-based techniques. The most widely applied form of soils washing, that employed by Bergmann and described here, is an *ex situ* water-based volume reduction process using particle size separation.

The underlying principle employed in soils washing is the well documented fact that contaminants have greatest affinity for the fine particles, the silts and clays, in a soil or sediment. This affinity is the effect of surface attractive forces, and the high surface area-to-volume ratio of the small particles. The principle applies across a wide range of contaminant types from heavy metals to hydrocarbons to organochlorines. This accounts for the wide applicability of soils washing across different site types (gas works, fuel storage, chemical plants, metal finishing) and, most importantly, enables the technique to be applied successfully to real sites where the contamination is complex and a cocktail of different contaminants is encountered.

It must be emphasized that soils washing is in itself not a complete treatment or destruction process for contaminated soils or sediments. It is rather a volume reduction step intended to recover a substantial portion of the original volume as cleaned, for re-use or easy low cost disposal, with a greatly reduced volume of contaminated material still requiring further treatment or safe disposal. This volume reduction can make the on-site treatment of contaminated land more manageable, reduce costs and enable a range of more expensive treatment technologies to be applied to the smaller volume of residual contamination.

As a generalization, if soils washing is to prove cost effective on a given site, it should be possible to recover 70–90% of the mass of feed material as cleaned, leaving 10–30% as contaminated residue (see Figure 3.1). If the recovery of cleaned product drops much below 70%, it is unlikely that the application of soils washing will be justified.

The main process step in a Bergmann soils washing plant is particle size separation using hydrocyclone separators. Typically the bulk of the contaminants will be found in the fine particles below a point in the range 45–70 microns. Having established the appropriate cut point for a specific soil or sediment, a hydrocyclone separator configuration can be prepared to achieve this separation.

From this, it is clear that the particle size characteristics of the soil or sediment will largely determine the relative proportions of cleaned coarse product and contaminated fines, and hence the cost-effectiveness of soils washing. As a generalization, coarse soils or sediments (sandy soils, made ground with gravel, ash and clinker) will show greater potential for soils washing than silt or clay-based soils. This generalization should, however, be treated with caution, as experience shows that most sites which are of concern are those where potential for contaminant migration exists. Even if the underlying soil is clay, clean-up efforts are directed at the contaminated sandy soils or made ground nearer the surface.

Figure 3.2 shows the effect of particle size distribution on potential cleaned product recovery. Soil A is very sandy and if a cut point of 63 microns is found to be appropriate, approximately 10% of the particles are smaller than this and deemed to be contaminated. 90% is potentially available for recovery in the cleaned coarse product. Soil B is made up of very fine particles and with

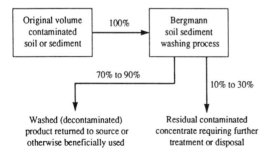

Figure 3.1   The principle of soils washing.

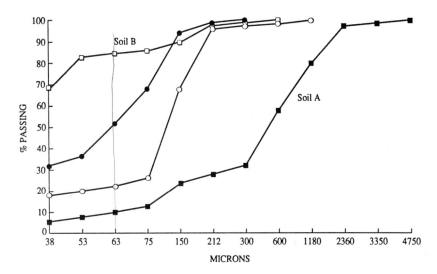

Figure 3.2   Particle size distribution for different soil types.

a cut point also at 63 microns, it can be seen that the potential cleaned product recovery is only 15%. Soils washing will be most unlikely to prove cost effective. In practice, the particle size distribution falls in between these extremes and also varies across a site. A feasibility study for soils washing should therefore consider all representative data from site investigations. If not carried out as a routine, sieve analysis should be performed on all trial pit or borehole samples taken as part of that site investigation.

SOILS WASHING PROCESS STEPS

The main process employed in a soils washing plant is particle size separation by hydrocyclone. This should, however, only be considered as the central element of a plant comprising a large number of process steps tailored to a specific application. The process steps employed in a typical Bergmann soils washing plant are:

- screening;
- attrition scrubbing;
- hydrocyclone separation;
- dense medium separation;
- gravity settling;
- dissolved air flotation;

- mechanical dewatering.

These process steps and their interactions are described in more detail in what follows. This list is not exhaustive, however, and other processes may be added if experience or the results of treatability studies show that they are required for removal of specific contaminants or contaminated particles. For example, additional processes such as crushing, upward flow classification, froth flotation, density spirals or activated carbon may be considered for specific duties.

The selected range of physical separation processes may operate with water alone as the wash medium, or chemical aids may be used to enhance performance by improving separation and removal of specific contaminants. The selection of chemical aids, if appropriate, is made on the basis of preliminary treatability studies, and is site specific. Typically those considered are pH adjustment, detergents, surfactants, chelating agents, oxidizing agents, coagulants and flocculants.

Returning to the 'typical' soils washing plant and the process steps employed (Figure 3.3), the plant may be considered in three parts:

- feed preparation;
- soils washing;
- water treatment.

FEED PREPARATION

The objective in this first section of the plant is to produce a classified feed for the soils washing plant proper, from the material as excavated or dredged. Scalping for the removal of large non-soil debris, wood, metal, etc, is carried out on a grizzly deck or primary vibrating screen. A wet rotary or vibrating screen, typically with an aperture size of 6 mm, is then used to reject oversize particles which will normally only have superficial contamination. After washing by high pressure sprays on the screen (possibly with chemical aids), the oversize particles can be recovered as cleaned. The wash water and particles of less than 6 mm diameter pass through the screen and enter the soils washing section of the plant[3].

SOILS WASHING

The classified slurry feed containing particles of less than 6 mm is delivered to a multi-stage attrition scrubber where contaminated silts and clays are detached from the surface of coarser particles and transferred into the wash water by a

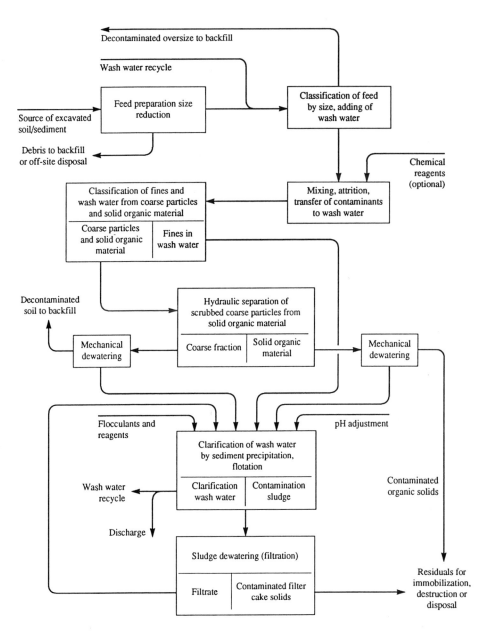

Figure 3.3   Typical soils washing plant flow diagram.

combination of:

• mechanical and shear stress caused by the vigorous interaction of granular particles induced by the rotating impellers within the attrition cells;

• addition of appropriate chemical aids which will promote the dissolution and transfer of contaminants from the surface of granular particles into the wash water.

The next step is to separate the contaminated fine particles (silts and clays) from the scrubbed granular material. Single or multi-stage hydrocyclone separators usually perform this function. Such separators yield two products:

• a substantially dewatered solids stream consisting principally of scrubbed granular particles with associated coarse organic particles such as coal, lignite, wood, etc;

• a stream comprising wash water with contaminated fines.

The solid organic particles associated with the scrubbed granular product usually represent only a small part of the total volume, but their organic nature leads to a high level of absorption of contaminants, usually requiring that these particles be removed if clean-up targets are to be achieved.

These solid organic particles can be efficiently removed in a form of dense medium separator which has been specifically developed for this purpose. Lighter organic particles (specific gravity (SG) of 1.8 or less) are 'floated' from a fluidized bed of the granular and more dense material (SG of 2.6 or higher). The isolated organic fraction is mechanically dewatered and forms part (albeit a small volume) of the contaminated residue from the plant requiring further treatment or disposal.

The cleaned and graded coarse product from the underflow of the dense medium separator may be given a final rinse and/or is dewatered using a vibrating screen.

WATER TREATMENT

The contaminated fines suspended in wash water arising from the various separation steps pass to the water treatment section of the plant. The objective here is to separate the solid particles and minimize the volume of the resulting sludge. In addition, chemical treatments may be applied to remove dissolved contaminants from the wash water (eg, pH increase to precipitate dissolved metals as hydroxides).

A combination of gravity sedimentation and dissolved air flotation are commonly used to separate the fines and any precipitation products from the wash water. Coagulants and flocculants may be used to enhance these separation processes. The resulting sludge represents the bulk of the residual contamination from the plant, and its volume should be reduced as much as is possible or economically achievable. Typically a stirred picket fence or deep cone thickener is used to produce a concentrated slurry which is fed to a mechanical dewatering device (belt press or centrifuge).

The treated wash water is recycled to the sumps and washed screens at the plant inlet. In the case of a relatively dry soil there is no wash water discharge from the plant, in fact a small continuous water make-up is required. With a dredged sediment, where the initial water content is much higher, there will be a liquid effluent discharge. In these cases the water treatment processes employed must be capable of meeting standards set down to discharge to sewer or watercourse.

PRODUCTS FROM SOILS WASHING

The solid products from a soils washing plant will typically be:

• rubble and large debris items;

• washed oversize (6 mm) particles from screen;

• filter cake (60–65% dry solids (DS)) of contaminated fines for further treatment or disposal;

• solid contaminated organics dewatered to 60–80% DS (small volume);

• dewatered cleaned coarse particles.

The last of these should represent the largest product volume. Typically dewatered to 85% DS or more, this cleaned graded coarse product is easily handled, stockpiled and transported.

EXAMPLES OF SOILS WASHING APPLICATIONS

The effect of volume reduction by soils washing on clean-up costs can be illustrated by examples drawn from recent investigations on two UK sites. The first is a large site with former mixed industrial use where 300,000 m^3 of soil contaminated with heavy metals and hydrocarbons is to be treated. The second is an example of the application of soils washing to the processing of dredged sediments. A small harbour containing 20,000 m^3 of polychlorinated biphenyl (PCB) contaminated sediments is to be dredged. The level of PCB contamination is such that the dredgings cannot be returned to the sea and must be treated or disposed of on land.

EXAMPLE 1

300,000 m³ of contaminated soil from a mixed industrial use site. The soil is contaminated with heavy metals and hydrocarbons which are present at a wide range of concentrations.

From the site investigation report and a subsequent laboratory-based treatability study, it was established that:

- *In situ* SG of soil = 1.9, DS content = 78%.
- 73% (by weight DS) <6 mm.
- 19% (by weight DS) <63 micron.
- Primary separation at 63 micron gave residual contamination in cleaned coarse product below limits set for re-use on site.
- Contaminated fines SG = 2.
- Filter cake dryness = 70% DS.

From this data, it can be calculated that 300,000 m³ of soil excavated weighs 570,000 t, or 444,600 t on a dry solids basis, of which:

- 120,042 t is larger than 6 mm and recovered as washed oversize from the screens at the inlet to the soils washing plant.
- 240,084 t is between 6 mm and 63 micron and will be recovered as cleaned, dewatered to approximately 80% DS.
- 84,474 t is contaminated fines (smaller than 63 micron), and will be separated and dewatered to produce approximately 78 500 m³ of filter cake for further treatment or disposal.

In this case, the plant was selected to enable processing of the total volume over a 20 month contract period — to match the rate of excavation, handling and reinstatement of material from the site. The rate limiting step in this case is fines separation and dewatering. A plant with a fines rating of 15 tonnes per hour (tph) (DS basis), working 80 hours per week and assuming 90% availability will complete the work in the 20 months allowed. If a shorter processing period is required, a larger plant or extended operating hours can be considered, in which case the economics will need to be reassessed.

The total cost of establishment on site and operation of a soils washing plant for this duty was calculated as £3.3m. This includes all costs associated with the soils washing plant: mobilization and lease charges, commissioning, operator training, supervision, labour, power, chemicals (in this case a signifi-cant cost item as a result of the mixed contamination present), dismantling on completion and removal from site. The £3.3m figure does not include cost of excavation and transport of material to the plant, nor disposal of the products and residues. It can be seen that the cost of soils washing equates to £11/m^3 which is found to be a not-untypical figure for relatively large sites where processing can take place over a reasonably long period of time.

It is now possible to compare the cost of disposal or treatment by some other method, with the combined costs of soils washing and treatment or disposal of the contaminated residues. Figure 3.4 overleaf illustrates the cost benefits of volume reduction.

There is some over-simplification in this analysis. For example, it is assumed that the oversized debris and cleaned coarse product from the soils washing plant may be re-used on site, used beneficially elsewhere or disposed of at zero cost. Also, no allowance has been made for reduction of clean fill imports which may arise from re-use of the cleaned material.

Figure 3.4 shows that unless the contaminated soils from this site can be taken to landfill or comprehensively treated for less than £15/m^3, then soils washing first will reduce overall costs. Once disposal or other treatment costs rise to £25/m^3, the savings are considerable (approximately £2.2m or 29%).

EXAMPLE 2

20,000 m^3 of contaminated sediments to be dredged from a small harbour. The dredgings will be contaminated with PCB at a level which will prevent disposal at sea and require treatment or disposal on land.

Data gathered from initial survey and subsequent treatability study:

- *In situ* SG = 1.3, DS content = 45%.
- As dredged SG = 1.2, DS content = 30% DS.
- 84% (by weight DS) mm.
- 28% (by weight DS) 5 micron.
- Primary separation at 53 micron gave residual contamination in cleaned coarse product below target levels.
- Contaminated fines SG = 1.8.
- Filter cake dryness = 65% DS.

20,000 m^3 *in situ* weighs 26,000 t and of this the dry solids content is 11,700 t. When dredged this will bulk up to:

$$\frac{11\,700}{0.3 \times 1.2} = 32\,500 \text{ m}^3$$

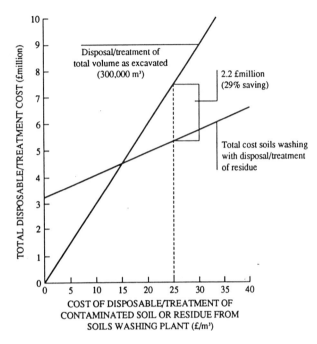

Figure 3.4.   Cost-effectiveness of soils washing. Example 1 Industrial land.

If 50% of the water 'added' during the dredging is allowed to drain away before disposal or treatment, the volume becomes 26,250 m³. In practice it may not be possible to reduce the volume for disposal in this way, as the water draining from the dredgings may be deemed to be contaminated and not suitable for discharge.

Of the 11,700 t of solids:

• 1,872 t is larger than 6 mm and recovered as washed oversize from the screens at the inlet to the soils washing plant.

• 6,552 t is between 6 mm and 53 micron, and will be recovered as cleaned, dewatered to approximately 80% DS.

• 3,276 t is contaminated fines and will be separated and dewatered to produce approximately 3,600 m³ of filter cake for further treatment or disposal.

In this case the plant was selected to enable processing of the total volume over a 3 month period, the plant having a capacity of 7 tph of fines, and operating 40 hours/week, with an assumed 90% availability.

The total cost of establishment and operation of a soils washing plant

SOILS WASHING

for this duty is calculated as £290,000 on the same basis as used in Example 1. This equates to a cost of £14.50/m³ of *in situ* volume or £8.90/m³ as dredged.

Again, it is possible to compare the treatment and disposal costs with and without volume reduction by soils washing (Figure 3.5). An important assumption here is that the unit disposal cost of as dredged material and filter cake from the soils washing plant will be the same. In practice, the 'as dredged' material will be in slurry form and consequently more difficult to transport and apply to landfill. For this reason a premium will usually be applied to the disposal cost, further enhancing the cost saving obtainable with soils washing.

This analysis compares disposal as dredged (or after allowing 50% of 'added' water to drain away) with soils washing and disposal of residue. It can be seen that unless disposal can be achieved for less than £10–£13/m³, soils washing will reduce overall cost. At £25/m³ soils washing will show a saving of £270,000–£430,000 (42–54%). This demonstrates that this technology is particularly cost-effective with dredged sediments with the benefit gained from dewatering of both cleaned coarse product and contaminated residues.

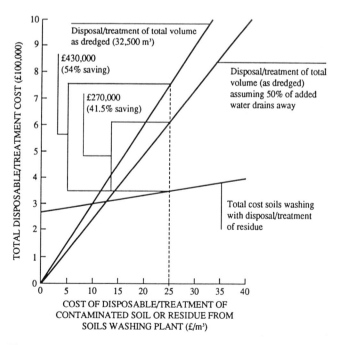

Figure 3.5.   Cost-effectiveness of soils washing. Example 2 Dredged sediment.

45

CLEAN-UP STANDARDS

Typical contaminant groups which may be effectively dealt with by soils washing include:

- petroleum and fuel residues;
- heavy metals;
- polychlorinated biohenyls (PCBs);
- polyaromatic hydrocarbons (PAHs);
- pesticides;
- creosote;
- cyanides;
- radioactive materials;
- asbestos.

An important question when evaluating the potential for the use of soils washing on a specific site is the level of clean-up which can be achieved (ie, what is the residual contaminant concentration in the cleaned coarse product?). The predicted residual contamination will have to be compared with standards set for re-use on site, or for low cost disposal, in order to establish whether soils washing is a practical proposition.

Very high contaminant removal efficiencies (99% or greater) have been achieved with commercial soils washing plants. Clean-up performance is, however, site specific and dependent upon the physical/chemical characteristics of the soil or sediment and the nature, disposition and concentration of contaminants present. To predict reliably whether specific targets for residual contamination can be met, a treatability study based in the laboratory will usually be required or, for major or very complex projects, on-site tests may be conducted using transportable pilot plant equipment.

In general, clean-up performance will be enhanced by use of chemical aids to the various separation processes employed in the soils washing plant. In many cases, however, water washing alone will be effective and, if targets for residual contamination can be met without use of chemicals, the economics of soils washing will be further improved. Typical chemical aids may include surfactants or detergents to remove superficial oil contamination from coarse particles, or pH reduction to force heavy metals into solution.

In most real sites with mixed contamination (perhaps hydrocarbons and one or more heavy metals) it may be necessary to adopt a compromise combining soils washing with chemical treatment, so that acceptable results are obtained across the whole spectrum of contaminants present. It follows that the highest clean-up performance can be achieved on sites with a single contaminant, because the plant operation, and any chemical aids used may be directed at that one contaminant.

Much of the operational experience with soils washing comes from Holland, where a number of large installations have been operating for many years, processing soils and dredged sediments from a wide range of contaminated sites. In most cases, the cleaned product is re-used on site, or for some beneficial use such as road making, or as general fill. The requirement is normally to reduce the level of residual contamination substantially below the 'B level' of the Dutch Standards. In most cases, given a suitable soil or sediment type, soils washing readily and consistently meets this requirement. Tables 3.1 and 3.2 provide a compilation of results from operating plants compared with the Dutch B level. All of this data comes from processing material from mixed contamination sites; even lower concentrations can be obtained by more precise targeting of contaminants on less complex sites.

TABLE 3.1

Typical soils washing performance data: inorganic metal contamination

Contaminant	Dutch standard (mg/kg)		Before	After
	B	C		
Cr	250	800	100–2500	70–120
			110–320	3
			184	64
			43–45	11–15
Ni	100	500	250–890	40–70
			100–600	50–80
Zn	500	3000	6040	150
			460–720	140–200
			160–170	50–80
Pb	150	600	11900	110
			110–450	20–70
			1450	20
Hg	2	10	67	1.5
			67	1.4
As	30	50	135	19
			180	3
Cd	5	20	3000–18000	20
			4–18	0.5–1.4

TABLE 3.2

Typical soils washing performance data: organic contaminants

Contaminant	Dutch standard (mg/kg)		Before	After
	B	C		
Mineral oil	1000	5000	6000	<20
			273–933	<20
CN (total)	50	500	75–300	7–10
			400–1000	6–10
			250–500	10–15
PCBs	1	10	2–4	0.1–0.2
Oil			19600	334
			233	<20
			3000–18000	20
PCAs (total)	20	200	250–400	0.5–10
			79	7.9
			19	0.34
			638	7.8
Chlorinated hydrocarbons	1	10	20–30	<1
			5.3	0.4

THE ROLE OF DEMONSTRATION PROJECTS

In North America, Bergmann USA has in the past 18 months participated in two major high-profile demonstration projects. Such projects enable the effectiveness of technologies such as soils washing to be demonstrated and costs to be evaluated. Usually linked with either central or local government funding, the result is that data generated by these projects is widely disseminated and available for review by others faced with cleaning up similar contaminated sites.

Final reports on both of these recent North American demonstration projects have yet to be published. However, brief details and some results are included here[4,5].

THE TORONTO HARBOUR COMMISSIONERS' SOIL RECYCLING DEMONSTRATION PROJECT

A large area of land in the port Industrial District of Toronto has effectively been unavailable for development as a result of contamination arising from its former mixed industrial use. The Toronto Harbour Commissioners arranged a study to determine whether it would be feasible to construct and operate a full-scale soil recycling facility. The study conducted by SNC Inc under the direction of Dr Diana Mourato concluded that such a recycling facility was feasible, and the

Toronto Harbour Commissioners asked SNC to set up a large-scale demonstration of those technologies which had been identified in the study.

The background to this project is interesting and serves to highlight differences between UK and Canada in legislation and in economic factors affecting contaminated land reclamation. Licensed landfills in the area will only accept soil lightly contaminated with hydrocarbons. When off-site disposal is available, the costs (at the time of the study) were in the order of $200/t. The aim of the demonstration project was, therefore, to assess whether the contaminated soil could be treated sufficiently by a combination of technologies, to allow the bulk of the material to be retained on site.

Bergmann USA designed, supplied and operated a 5–10 tph soils washing plant to perform the initial clean material recovery and volumetric reduction of the contaminants. The contaminated product was then processed by innovative metal extraction and biodegration technologies.

During the demonstration project the Bergmann USA soils washing plant processed some 3,000 t of heavy metal, PAH, polynuclear aromatic (PNA) and petroleum hydrocarbon contaminated material.

During April and May 1992 a SITE (Superfund Innovative Technology Evaluation Programme) demonstration was carried out when the soils washing plant was processing soils from an area formerly used for metal finishing and refinery and petroleum storage.

Results from the SITE demonstration are summarized in Tables 3.3 (a) and (b) overleaf.

The Toronto Harbour demonstration tests found that soils washing produced two products (washed oversize from screens and cleaned coarse particles) with contamination levels significantly reduced in comparison with the feed soil. In addition, the contaminants were found to be concentrated primarily in the contaminated slurry which was then routed for further processing.

SAGINAW BAY DEMONSTRATION
This demonstration project was also conducted as part of the SITE programme with additional investigations carried out by US Army Corps of Engineers (USACE). The site of the demonstration was the USACE Confined Disposal Facility in the Saginaw Bay of Lake Huron. The feed 'soil' for the SITE demonstration tests consisted of sediments which had previously been dredged from the Saginaw River. The 'soil' was contaminated with low levels of PCBs

TABLE 3.3

Comparison of feed concentration with cleaned coarse and contaminated fine products from two North American demonstration projects

(a) Toronto Harbour

Description of contaminant	Feed	Cleaned coarse product	Contaminated fines product
Oil and grease	8330	2180	40,000
TRPH*	2540	621	14,000
Copper	16.9	13.8	80.9
Lead	115	46.0	520
Zinc	82.5	34.1	329
Naphthalene	11.2	2.05	51.7
Phenanthrene	6.91	1.77	34.7
Pyrene	5.06	1.43	26.3
Benzo(a)pyrene	1.91	0.53	10.0

Total recoverable petroleum hydrocarbons   All in mg/kg

(b) Saginaw Bay

Conditions	Feed	Cleaned coarse product	Contaminated fines product
5 day mean (no surfactant)	1.27	0.188	4.53
1 day mean (surfactant added)	1.57	0.189	3.68

and heavy metals from industrial activities along the Saginaw River.

The plant used for the demonstrations was rated at some 4 tph and the main particle size separation was performed with a cut point of 45 micron. During a four-day test (continuous operation over 8 hours each day) the performance without the use of surfactant as an aid to the washing process was monitored. A selection of the results relating to PCB concentrations is shown in Tables 3.3 (a) and (b). In a second test over one day, the plant was operated under the same conditions with a surfactant added (Moncosolve 210). Little difference in performance was found, illustrating that with relatively low initial contaminant concentration, the additional cost of this chemical treatment can be avoided. In cases where the feed concentrations are much higher, surfactant use will increase the plant's ability to distribute organic contaminants into the appropriate output streams by solubilizing and removing organics from the washed sediments.

Some of the conclusions drawn from the SITE evaluation were:

• The process can successfully separate the grains smaller than 45 micron from the input soil/sediment and concentrate them into the output fines, producing two other streams of clean sand and gravel and a humic (solid organic) fraction.

• Organic contaminants (PCB in this case) are concentrated in the output fines and the humic fraction.

• The largest output stream is the clean sand and gravel, the mass of this product being a function of the grain size distribution in the feed.

• The concentration of the organic contaminants (PCB) in the clean coarse fraction was approximately 87.5% lower than in the feed.

• The on-line factor of the plant is high, during the 5×8 hour/day test being 100%.

The value of demonstration projects like these is unquestionable. Demonstration projects enable a large-scale assessment of technologies to be made for a specific site, provide a platform for the introduction of new technologies, and give direction and confidence for those faced with cleaning up similar sites. In particular the Toronto project illustrates the possibility for development and evaluation of an integrated suite of treatment technologies to effect complete treatment on site. Manufacturers and technology producers should welcome the opportunity to participate in demonstration projects and it is to be hoped that a number of such projects will be seen in the UK in the next few years.

CONCLUSIONS

This chapter has set out the principles and main process elements employed in the most widely-applied form of soils washing. The effect of volume reduction on overall treatment/disposal costs has been quantified, and the question of 'how clean' has been addressed. The application of soils washing to dredged sediments, where cost savings from volume reduction can be significantly higher, should not be overlooked.

Soils washing offers a means of making site reclamation more manageable and cost effective. The most straightforward application to consider is the reduction in volume of contaminated material to be transported off site for landfill disposal. In the majority of cases studied to date, with more than

10,000 m^3 of contaminated soil, soils washing can be justified on economic grounds based upon current transport and landfill costs. If, as widely predicted, these costs rise in the future, the economic case will become stronger, and to this can be added non-financial benefits such as reduced vehicle movements.

Even if the intention is to retain contaminated material on the site in suitably engineered containment, soils washing may be worth considering in order to reduce the volume of that containment with savings in construction and future control and monitoring costs.

Most importantly, however, soils washing has a growing role to play as part of an integrated suite of treatment technologies on contaminated sites. Volume reduction by soils washing provides a concentrated feed stock in slurry or dewatered cake form for downstream treatment or destruction techniques such as incineration, vitrification, *ex situ* biotreatment and metal extraction. It is becoming widely accepted that a single technology solution rarely exists for on-site treatment. Some treatment processes may be impractical because of variability in conditions and contaminant distribution across a site or simply prohibitively expensive if used to process the entire excavated volume. Soils washing can therefore be considered as an enabling step, making the overall reclamation project more manageable and lowering combined treatment costs in an integrated treatment programme to the point where this can be economically attractive, as well as desirable compared to off-site disposal.

REFERENCES
1. Timothy, S., 1992, *Contaminated Land: Market and Technology Issues*, (Centre for Exploitation of Science and Technology).
2. Armishaw, R., Bardos, R.P., Dunn, R.M., Hill, J.M., Pearl, M., Rampling, T. and Wood, P.A., 1992, *Review of Innovative Contaminated Soil Clean-Up Processes*, (Warren Spring Laboratory).
3. Ennis, R.E., *Advanced Physical/Chemical Techniques for The Remediation of Contaminated Soils*, (Conference Proceedings), (Bergmann, USA).
4. Mourato, D. and Lang, D., 1992, *The Toronto Harbour Commissioners' Soils Recycling Demonstration Project*, (Conference Proceedings).
5. *The Superfund Innovative Technology Evaluation Programme, Bergmann U.S.A., Soil/Sediment Washing Technology, Applications Analysis Report* (Draft), October 1992, US Environmental Protection Agency.

4. BIOLOGICAL REMEDIATION: A EUROPEAN PERSPECTIVE

Jos Verheul, Peter de Bruijn and Susan Herbert

The Netherlands has taken a proactive approach to contaminated land and its remediation for many years. This reflects a strong commitment to environmental matters generally. It also results from a heavy reliance on groundwater resources for public water supplies in a situation where the groundwater table is very close to ground surface and hence very susceptible to pollution by surface activities. Over 100,000 suspected contaminated sites have been identified in the Netherlands to date, of which some 25% are thought to pose a significant threat to public health or the environment[1]. Some 80,000 of the total number of suspected sites are former industrial sites, whilst 25,000 are current industrial sites. Approximately 3,000 are recorded as landfill sites.

Major experience in the Netherlands of soil and groundwater investigation and remediation of contamination covers a period of more than 10 years. In particular, valuable experience has been gained in the fields of policy and regulation, techniques and strategies for investigations, clean-up and control remedial measures, processing of solid and liquid residuals as well as general 'facts of life' lessons.

This chapter focuses on the development of biological treatment of contaminated soil and groundwater. Biological treatment methods use micro-organisms to break down, modify or destroy contaminants through their natural enzymatic activities. The technology is potentially applicable to a wide range of organic contaminants and soil types, and to treatment of contaminated water. Biological treatment can be carried out either *ex situ*, ie after removal of the contaminated soil or water from the ground, or *in situ*, ie without removal or excavation.

For several years, there has been considerable interest in the biological treatment of soil and groundwater and its possibilities for the remediation of contamination. However, a real breakthrough in terms of availability in the commercial market has not yet been achieved. Out of all remediated contaminated soil in the Netherlands in 1991, only a few percent was treated biologically, and the proportion which used *in situ* biological treatment is too small to mention. The same situation applies to biological treatment of groundwater; groundwater is more normally treated mainly by physical or chemical methods. This low level of use of biological remediation reflects principally the difficulty of achieving the required Dutch 'A' level, the reference value below which soils or water are probably uncontaminated, using biological treatment. Nevertheless, a great effort is being made in the Netherlands to improve all techniques of biological treatment, for soil as well as groundwater.

This chapter describes the development of landfarming, *in situ* bioremediation and a new type of bioreactor for the treatment of groundwater, using case histories from the Netherlands and experiences from other countries. Initially, however, we comment on the European approach to remediation of contaminated land, as undertaken in the Netherlands and Germany.

THE REMEDIAL APPROACH AND TECHNIQUES IN THE NETHERLANDS
The Dutch Ministry of Housing, Physical Planning and the Environment has defined contaminated land as:

'Land where substances are present in soil at concentrations higher than those in which they would normally expect to occur and where they pose a serious threat to public health and the environment.'

The approach towards contaminated land in the Netherlands is based on the concept of multi-functionality. This requires the protection of soil resources to ensure that they remain capable of supporting any end-use, including agriculture and horticulture. This contrasts with the approach adopted in the UK, where remediation of contaminated land is related to land use, with higher standards of remedial treatment required for more sensitive end-uses such as residential, than those for less sensitive uses such as industrial or hard cover.

The Netherlands differs from the UK also in that it has legislated specifically for contaminated land. Policy was initiated in the late sixties and early seventies and a draft Soil Protection Act was developed in 1972. This was not entered into the statute books, however, and formal legislation related to contaminated soil did not exist until the 1980s. Nowadays, however, in addition to the Soil Protection Act of 1987 which aims to prevent the deposition of specified substances and hence reduce the incidence of future contamination, the Interim Soil Clean-up Act of 1982 provides the necessary administrative and financial resources to identify and treat historically contaminated sites. Soil quality standards, the so-called Dutch ABC levels, were introduced to assist in classifying sites suspected of contamination and to aid ascribing priority to sites requiring remedial action. These ABC values are legally binding for assessment and remediation of contaminated sites, although in practice there is some flexibility in the application of the values, particularly in highly industrialized areas. The ABC values are under constant review by the Dutch Authorities and at present the A levels are being replaced by 'reference values' which will take into account soil properties when defining background levels of contamination.

None of the legislation provided a basis for a systematic and comprehensive inventory and registration of all potentially contaminated sites, however, and the early attempts by different provinces to prepare a registration scheme led to wide variations in approach in different parts of the Netherlands. To redress this situation, and to allow Dutch industry control over the planning and timescale of remediation, the Dutch enterprises organization (VNO), in co-operation with central government, took the initiative in 1987 and developed a programme for the voluntary registration, investigation and remediation of contaminated sites. Whilst the question of financing remediation is still problematic, the issue of registration has not provoked the level of concern experienced in the UK and, indeed, is seen to offer a number of advantages[2].

Dutch policy includes recognition of the 'polluter pays' principle, although the Dutch have taken a more pragmatic approach and state funding has been provided in the first instance for remediation of contaminated land, with powers to recover costs from the responsible parties at a later date.

THE GERMAN APPROACH

German policies on contaminated land have developed over recent years in response to specific contaminated land incidents and now two different categories of contaminated land are recognized: former industrial sites and abandoned waste disposal sites. A survey[3] during 1990 estimated that the total number of contaminated sites within the whole of Germany (after reunification) was over 150,000. The German Federal Environment Agency has defined contaminated land as:

'Land that presents a potential direct or indirect adverse impact upon the health and welfare of human and economically important natural resources such as livestock, crops and groundwater sources.'

There are currently no agreed national soil or groundwater standards which apply in Germany, although the Federal Environment Agency is attempting to establish some. The responsibility for dealing with contaminated sites lies with the federal state authorities, and so there are variations between the approach adopted in different parts of the country. The Dutch ABC levels are used in some areas, although when using these, the evaluation is required to take account of the local situation — eg land use, regulatory requirements, etc — when deciding on remedial action. In general the Germans have adopted a three-stage approach for the remediation of contaminated land:

* stage 1 — registration of potentially contaminated sites;
* stage 2 — investigation and assessment;
* stage 3 — remediation.

REMEDIAL OPTIONS

Clean-up and control of contamination can be undertaken by a number of different techniques, including:

Clean-up:

* civil engineering techniques: excavation including supportive geotechnical measures and drainage;
* consequential disposal or treatment of contaminated soil;
* groundwater clean-up: withdrawal and processing of contaminated ground-water, optionally including infiltration, etc;
* *in situ* treatment, including soil-air extraction and stripping, bioremediation, electro-reclamation and extraction by flushing.

Isolation and control:

* hydraulic isolation, optionally including supportive geotechnical measures;
* physical isolation by the installation of barriers (horizontal, vertical), optionally including hydraulic control measures;
* immobilization techniques, eg solidification and stabilization;
* additional technical and non-technical control measures (monitoring, inspection and maintenance, organizational framework, scheme planning/layout).

Excavation and subsequent disposal off site of contaminated soils has been widely used historically in the Netherlands, although this does not really solve the larger problem of contaminated land since it involves moving the contaminated material somewhere else. Subsequently constraints were applied in the Netherlands to remediation: if technically feasible and within specific cost limits treatment is required. Treatment usually consists of one of the following options:

* thermal treatment;

- extractive treatment;
- microbiological treatment.

Table 4.1 gives a brief summary of the applicability of these treatments to different soil types and Table 4.2 relates in general terms the treatment to contaminant types.

The costs of treatment differ according to soil type and type of contaminant(s). In general the following ranges apply in the Netherlands today:

Thermal   Dfl 100–200/ton
Extractive   Dfl 100–200/ton
Landfarming   Dfl 80–130/ton

(at a conversion rate of Dfl 2.65 to the pound).

By using thermal and extractive treatments, contaminated soil can be cleaned to a significant extent. With landfarming and *in situ* biological remediation techniques comparable results can theoretically be achieved. This can not be guaranteed, however, and depends strongly on soil type, contaminant, processing time and conditions, and thus indirectly on costs.

Groundwater clean-up operations were started optimistically on the basis of relatively short anticipated periods (a few months) for treatment. In general the time period required for remediation is much longer — of the order

TABLE 4.1

Treatment techniques related to soil type

Treatment	Soil type				
	Sandy (low organic carbon)	Sandy (high organic carbon)	Silt and clay	Peat	Hetero-geneous
Extractive	+	+/o	—	—/?	o
Thermal:					
low temperature	+	+	+	+/o	+/o
high temperature	+	+	+	+	+
Landfarming/*in situ* biorestoration	+	+	—	o	o

+ = applicable in general
o = applicable in some cases
— = in general not applicable

TABLE 4.2

Treatment techniques related to contaminant types

Treatment	Contaminant			
	Heavy metals	**Cyanides**	**Complex cyanides**	**Volatile alifatics and aromatics**
Extractive	+	+	+	+
Thermal:				
low temperature	—	—	—	+
high temperature	—	—	o	+
Landfarming/*in situ* biorestoration	—	o/—	—	+

+ = applicable in general
o = applicable in some cases
— = in general not applicable
? = unknown

of many years. Hydrogeological characteristics and geochemical processes control the type and extent of contamination, and thus influence the design, operation and ultimate effectiveness of groundwater remediation techniques. At the present time, considerable effort is being given to optimizing efficiency and costs of the treatment process by geographic layout of extraction/infiltration wells, design of the withdrawal and infiltration system and operating procedures.

In situ remedial treatment techniques are promising, although practical, full-scale experience is limited. The advantages of *in situ* techniques where the remedial treatment can be implemented within the ground without excavation or abstraction of the contaminated soil or water are clearly numerous, particularly for operational industrial sites or those which are already occupied. Site-specific characteristics, including soil type and variety of contaminant, restrict the applicability of these techniques. The physical and hydrogeological properties of the soils in question, at different spatial scales, seem to be of utmost importance for success.

If clean-up or treatment is not considered to be feasible either technically and/or financially, isolation and control are alternative options for remediation of contamination. Basically the same techniques are applied for both options, although at different scales and with different aims. The aims of

TABLE 4.2 continued

Treatment techniques related to contaminant types

Treatment	Contaminant			
	Non-volatile alifatics and aromatics	Volatile chlorinated hydrocarbons	Non-volatile chlorinated hydrocarbons	Other
Extractive	+	+	+	+
Thermal:				
low temperature	o	o*	—	—
high temperature	+	o*	o	o
Landfarming/*in situ* biorestoration	+/o	—	—	o

* = depending on the type of installation, use of high temperature afterburner (>1200°C) is necessary

isolation are to minimize risks due to migration of contamination in the environment and/or exposure of relevant target groups. This is achieved by various techniques, according to the specific situation. Physical encapsulation or isolation by vertical barriers (steel, bentonite, HDPE or combination) or horizontal impermeable layers with complementary drainage facilities is regularly adopted. Similarly, hydraulic isolation and control systems are regularly used. These involve the same elements as groundwater clean-up systems, although applied at a more extensive operational level. At present in the Netherlands, immobilization techniques are rarely used for contaminated land remediation.

DHV'S R&D PROGRAMME

DHV Environmental Technology, our division of DHV Burrow-Crocker, has its own research and development programme for the development of new techniques for soil and groundwater remediation. As part of this programme there is close co-operation with university research institutes and contractors. Five techniques have been chosen for further development:

1. Landfarming.
2. *In situ* biorestoration.
3. Use of a bioreactor for groundwater treatment.

4. Soil-air analyses and extraction.
5. *In situ* bioremediation of trichloroethylene and tetrachloroethylene.

LANDFARMING

DHV is currently investigating two methods to improve the landfarm method, by so-called intensive landfarming and by dynamic landfarming techniques. On intensive landfarming, DHV is working in association with a local contractor. A pilot experiment (scale 15 m^3) on a sandy soil contaminated with diesel fuel is under way. The scope of the study is to improve the biodegradability of the contaminant by a new method for pretreatment of the soil and an intensive mixing of the soil during the landfarm period. All other parameters are optimized (pH, nutrients and aeration). It is expected that within a short period (2–3 months) the Dutch A level can be reached, depending on initial concentrations of contamination.

With dynamic landfarming, a dynamic equilibrium of soil-air, soil-water and soil is created by constructing a soilbank. A large-scale experiment is programmed for this technique in co-operation with the municipality of Amsterdam and with a funder. For this approach, the ultimate clean-up target is the Dutch A level.

IN SITU BIORESTORATION

In situ biorestoration is a well-known method, of which substantial experience has been gained in the USA and to a lesser extent in Germany. But the results of these overseas projects are sometimes difficult to interpret.

The advantages of this method are numerous, and clearly include the major advantage of eliminating the need for extensive disruption of the site. DHV started a full-scale project on *in situ* bioremediation at the end of 1990. It is expected that the site will be cleaned to a level between the A and B values. Although it involves a 'real-world' clean-up site, the project aims to obtain an insight into all practical aspects related to *in situ* biorestoration.

BIOREACTOR

In co-operation with the Agricultural University at Wageningen, a bioreactor has been developed for the purification of groundwater extracted during groundwater clean-up projects. Over a nine month period, a pilot study was carried out on the removal of volatile aromatics and naphthalene. This was very successful, with elimination capacities up to 100% measured. A full-scale project started in March 1993.

SOIL-AIR ANALYSES AND EXTRACTION

In co-operation with Hannover Milieu en Veiligheidstechniek (a Dutch firm specializing in soil venting) an investigation is being undertaken to establish a well-defined relationship between concentrations of contaminants in soil-air and concentrations in the soil. With the results of this, a computer model for the prediction of groundwater clean-up is to be adapted to predict efficiency and the time needed for soil venting.

IN SITU BIOREMEDIATION OF TRICHLOROETHYLENE AND TETRACHLORO-ETHYLENE

In co-operation with the University of Groningen, the Agricultural University at Wageningen, and the Dutch distributor for natural gas, DHV is investigating at pilot scale the *in situ* bioremediation of soils and groundwater contaminated with trichloroethylene and tetrachloroethylene.

IN SITU BIOREMEDIATION

For several reasons *in situ* bioremediation (ISB) is not a 'proven technology'. The technique still needs a great deal of practical experience. Bioremediation does not guarantee the specific clean-up target (A level) as required by the Dutch government.

In 1990 DHV started an ISB of a petrol station site. The practical execution of an ISB was considered the only way to gain the knowledge and experience needed to develop this technique further. At this moment we can conclude that the groundwater clean-up has been successful. However, the clean-up of the soil has been only partly successful. Despite this, the knowledge that has been gained is of great value.

The site is a petrol station located at Velsen-Noord, which was renovated a few years ago, at which time it was found that the soil beneath the old part of the station was contaminated. The underlying soil consists of medium fine to medium coarse sand with horizontal and vertical permeabilities of 5 m/day and 1 m/day respectively. The groundwater level is about 1.2 m deep below ground level. The pollution consists mostly of gasoline caused by spillage and probably also from a leaking supply pipe. The soil has been contaminated from ground level to about 3–4 m deep.

The highest concentrations of contaminants measured in the soil during a detailed study were 2,690 mg/kg for mineral oil, and over 1,200 mg/kg for total aromatics (BTEX). The contaminated area totals about 250 m^2. This equates to around 1,500 tons of polluted soil. The highest concentrations measured in the groundwater were 16,000 µg/l for mineral oil and 65,000 µg/l for BTEX. The groundwater was polluted to a depth of at most 4–5 m below ground level. The total surface area of contaminated groundwater was around 1,200 m², and the total volume around 1,600 m³.

The contaminated soil within the unsaturated zone (to 1.3 m depth) was excavated and treated elsewhere. The remaining contaminated area (soil and groundwater) was treated by stimulating microbial degradation by adding oxygen and nutrients to recirculating groundwater. In view of the concentrations of contaminants in the soil and the relatively limited thickness of the contaminated layer, we decided to use vertical infiltration and withdrawal wells, flushing both the polluted soil and groundwater. In order to prevent migration of contaminated groundwater, the flow of the abstracted water exceeded the infiltration rate by 10% (12 m³/h against 11 m³/h). The surplus abstracted groundwater was discharged to the sewage system after treatment in a groundwater purification plant (GPP).

Nutrients were dosed from a central storage tank, where ammonium nitrate (NH_4NO_3) and monosodium dihydrogen phosphate (NaH_2PO_4) were dosed as solids and dissolved in tap water. The concentrations were approximately 2 mg/l ammonium, 3.5 mg/l nitrate and 12 mg/l phosphate.

Hydrogen peroxide was used as an oxygen source and was dosed from a storage tank with increasing concentrations from 10 to 100 mg/l.

Figure 4.1 shows a cross-section of the design of the remediation system.

The agreed clean-up target for both soil and groundwater was the Dutch B level (Table 4.3). However, in order to reach this level in the groundwater, a concentration level in the soil of A level (or even below) is required.

We started the remediation in November 1990. After one year of operation the remediation seemed to be a success except for the area directly beneath the pump island, where the highest concentration of contaminants had been recorded. Some results of the groundwater monitoring related to the A, B and C levels are summarized in Table 4.4 on page 64. The area beneath the pump island was subject to an intensive monitoring programme.

With respect to the contaminated soil the remediation was successful, except for the zone between 1.5 and 2.0 m depth beneath the pump island. Detailed analysis showed that the zone of 1.0–1.5 m depth was cleaned to below the A level. Below this, however, remarkably high concentrations persisted (up to 5,000 mg/kg). The reasons for this stagnation in the soil remediation could be

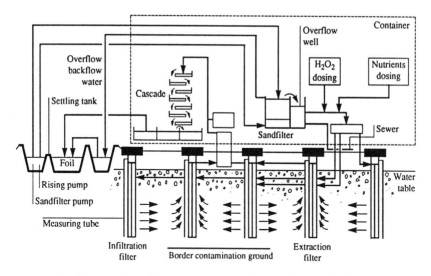

Figure 4.1   Cross-section of the groundwater purification plant and infiltration and extraction wells.

one (or a combination) of the following:

1.   A decrease in the regional groundwater level (from around 1.0 m depth to 1.5 m depth) left a layer of 0.5 m only slightly flushed.

2.   The initial concentrations in the soil were locally much higher than the levels used for the designing the remediation system.

THE COST OF BIOREMEDIATION

The costs of the project Velsen-Noord are summarized in Table 4.5. The first

TABLE 4.3

Dutch Standards (A, B and C level) for mineral oil and BTEX in soil and groundwater at the Velsen-Noord petrol station

	Dutch A level	Dutch B level	Dutch C level
Soil (mg/kg)			
mineral oil	50	1,000	5,000
BTEX	detection limit	7	70
Groundwater (μg/l)			
mineral oil	50	200	600
BTEX	detection limit	30	100

TABLE 4.4
Summarized results of the groundwater monitoring at Velsen-Noord

Monitoring well (1–4 m depth)	Nov 1990	May 1991	Sept 1991
Mineral oil			
monitoring 1	5×C	<A	<A
monitoring 2	6×C	A–B	<A
pump-island	4×C	3×C	3×C
BTEX			
monitoring 1	20×C	B	detection limit
monitoring 2	7×C	A–B	detection limit
pump-island	5×C	30×C	5×C

column shows the budget as expected initially in November 1989, and the second the actual expenses as established at 31 December 1991. The entry 'operating costs' covers the checking, maintenance and meetings as well as the costs of chemicals (around Dfl 17,000). This budget was overrun because of a much longer adjustment period for the installations than expected.

Total remediation costs amounted to Dfl 840,000, for which 1,450 tons of soil (850 m^3) as well as 2,000 m^3 of groundwater were cleaned up. This amounts to the approximated sum of Dfl 580/ton, including remediation and on-surface purification of the groundwater. When comparing the above costs with a conventional remediation technique, the financial implications are very

TABLE 4.5
Summary of the budgeted costs and actual expenditure — ISB location Velsen-Noord

Entry	Budget costs (Dfl) (November 1989)	Expenditure (Dfl) (December 1991)
1. Preparation	15,000	43,000
2. Design/construction	184,000	187,000
3. Investment costs	217,000	269,000
4. Operating costs	92,000	250,000
5. Monitoring/analysis	68,000	50,000
6. Reporting	20,000	41,000
Total 1–6	596,000	840,000

similar for both methods. It should be noted, however, that in the case of a total excavation approach the costs for demolishing, rebuilding and temporary closure should also be taken into account. Although the costs for the design stayed within budget, these costs are relatively high for an installation of this type and size. Future installations could be designed with a budget reduction of approximately 25%.

From the evaluation of the *in situ* biorestoration study at Velsen-Noord, the following conclusions can be drawn:

- The infiltration and withdrawal system functioned according to the design;

- The abstracted water could be purified very well with a simple GPP;

- To avoid limitation on the biodegradation by lack of oxygen, hydrogen peroxide is a satisfactory oxygen source;

- There is no need for a separate dosing system as hardly any decomposition took place in the pipeline;

- The groundwater clean-up was a success — even after a standstill it was confirmed that there was no new pollution;

- The clean-up of the polluted soil was partly successful due to a combination of lowered groundwater level and higher initial concentrations.

EXPERIENCES IN GERMANY AND THE USA

Investigation and application of *in situ* bioremediation has been studied in detail in both Germany and the USA. An international evaluation of *in situ* bioremediation was executed by the National Institute of Public Health and Environmental Protection. This section summarizes the experiences in Germany and the USA on the basis of around twenty case studies.

Bioremediation is mainly applied at service stations and at contaminated sites in the chemical industry. In the cases described the depth at which bioremediation was applied varied from 3 to 10 m below ground level. The soil mainly consisted of sand with permeabilities ranging from 1 up to 100 m/d. Contaminants were mainly gasoline and diesel fuel.

The approach to the design of an *in situ* bioremediation scheme was either from a microbiological viewpoint or from a hydrogeological one. A combination of the two disciplines was mentioned only exceptionally. A comprehensive site investigation and a laboratory investigation into the biodegradability of the contaminants decided whether *in situ* biorestoration was applicable or not. In some cases a pilot study was carried out.

The design of the system was in most cases quite simple, and consisted of infiltration and withdrawal wells, purification of the abstracted groundwater and addition of an oxygen source and nutrients. The groundwater purification plant consisted mainly of an oil/water separator, sand filtration and a stripping tower.

Hydrogen peroxide is widely used as an oxygen source and is usually the most efficient one. In only a few cases were air, pure oxygen or nitrate used. Addition of nutrients was mainly limited to nitrogen and phosphate.

Investigations and experiences involving the addition of surfactants showed only negative results. Experiences in the Netherlands also suggested that surfactants will not noticeably improve *in situ* bioremediation.

In some cases the site was inoculated with micro-organisms, but the applicability of this was not detailed in the results.

Although they are of considerable importance, only small attention was given in the case studies to monitoring strategies. A well-designed sampling and analysis programme is of major importance when *in situ* bioremediation is applied, particularly where the site is heterogeneous with respect to contaminants and soil structure.

Clean-up levels below the Dutch B level can be reached, according to the case study data. In some cases the A level was achieved. Clean-up time varied from three months up to four years. Both results and clean-up time will mainly depend on:

- the type and concentration of the contamination;
- the soil profile;
- the objectives of the clean-up.

No general estimates for costs can be given since these are strongly site-specific. Nevertheless, *in situ* bioremediation is considered to be a cost-effective and efficient method when applied to a suitable site.

EVALUATION OF BIOREMEDIATION

From these results, some general comments can be made to assist the decision on whether to use *in situ* bioremediation. Three main issues should be reviewed as a first stage:

1. Soil structure and hydrogeology

- heterogeneity of the subsoil
- permeabilities (horizontal and vertical)

- organic carbon content
- hydrogeological modelling of the site
2. Microbiology
- bacterial counts
- enrichment cultures
- biodegradation tests either in batches and/or soil columns
- if needed, for instance at complex sites: pilot investigation
3. Contamination
- comprehensive site investigation
- type of contaminants and concentration levels
- free-floating layers

In addition to these three main issues, attention should be given to geotechnical aspects such as settlement. It is important to realize that the unsaturated zone normally is not treatable by *in situ* bioremediation. Bioventing is usually a suitable alternative for the unsaturated zone.

LANDFARMING

The name 'landfarming' derives from agricultural practice. In the upper layers of agricultural soils the number of micro-organisms varies between 1 million and 1 billion per gram of soil. One to ten percent of this number has the potential to grow on hydrocarbons. Where roots penetrate into soil and produce root-exudates, the number of micro-organisms is large and their activity is high. By regularly ploughing the farmers maintain optimal environmental soil conditions for plant growth and decomposition of organic material.

Landfarming can thus be defined as a simple technique for bioremediation of polluted soil by applying good farming practice.

Biodegradation or bioremediation can be conveniently grouped in two categories, primary biodegradation (biotransformation) and ultimate biodegradation (mineralization). In this section, the following are considered:

- organic pollutants feasible for landfarming bioremediation;
- physical and chemical factors affecting the degradation;
- state of the art in the Netherlands;
- intensive landfarming;
- dynamic landfarming;
- landfarming of harbour sludge;

- advantages and limitations of the technique;
- the future of the technique.

Although all naturally produced organic compounds are suitable in principal for complete mineralization, in practice mainly hydrocarbons (like gasoline and diesel fuel) and some chlorinated organic compounds (eg hexachlorocyclohexane) have been tackled by the landfarming technique.

PHYSICAL AND CHEMICAL FACTORS AFFECTING THE DEGRADATION OF HYDROCARBONS

Hydrocarbons differ in their susceptibility to microbial attack and have been ranked in the following order of decreasing susceptibility:

- n-alkanes;
- branched alkanes;
- low molecular weight aromatics;
- cyclic alkanes;
- polycyclic aromatics.

Tarballs, slicks and large oil particles have a low surface-to-volume ratio, inhibiting microbial degradation since they restrict solubility of the components and access by micro-organisms. The formation of emulsions and the release of surfactants and biosurfactants is an important process in the uptake of hydrocarbons by bacteria, actonomycetes and fungi. Enhancing biodegradation by the application of detergents is an area not yet fully explored.

The rate of uptake and mineralization by microbial consortia are proportional to the available concentration, which is generally determined by the aqueous solubility.

There are thresholds of maximum and minimum concentrations. The latter may become 'invisible' while the former may become 'toxic' for the micro-organism or the enzyme. In particular volatile compounds may become toxic.

The available water limits microbial growth and metabolism. Optimal rates of biodegradation occur between 30% and 90% saturation.

Temperature influences the degradation rate by its effect on physical characteristics such as viscosity, volatilization and water solubility. Rates increase with increasing temperature. A basic 'design parameter' is therefore whether or not to manipulate temperature (plain open air landfarm, enhanced temperature by biological activity, landfarming in greenhouses). The average upper soil temperature in the Netherlands and England is 12–18°C between May and October, and even lower during other months.

For microbial degradation the hydrocarbon is the electron-donor and the electron-acceptor determines in which steps energy can be derived during the breakdown process. Oxygen, nitrate ions, manganese dioxide, iron oxides, sulphate ions and carbon dioxide are electron-acceptors. Oxygen is also necessary to become inserted into the molecule to be oxidized. Aerobic mineralization occurs at a faster rate than anaerobic. For the degradation of 1 g of oil, on average 3 g of oxygen is necessary. Lack of oxygen is often the rate limiting factor for oil degradation.

For growth of micro-organisms, in addition to a carbon source, other macro-elements are necessary such as N and P. The C:N:P ratio for optimal growth is generally 100:10:1. Maintaining optimal growth conditions implies taking into account the low solubility of phosphorus salts and the leachability of nitrogen salts.

Optimal rates of hydrocarbon degradation occur around a neutral pH. In acid soils an adjustment of pH is required. It often causes a shift in the dominant oil-decomposing populations.

THE STATE OF THE ART IN THE NETHERLANDS

In the Netherlands landfarming has been applied either *in situ* or on site, to sandy soils mainly, polluted with mineral oils. *In situ* treatment, where the soil is not removed, is restricted to the upper layer (with a maximum of approximately 40 cm) and is regularly cultivated according to a specific procedure. More frequently the on-site method has been used. In this case, polluted soil is removed and after separation of big particles and homogenization, is spread under controlled conditions in layers up to 80 cm thickness. Several firms are active in this field, each with their own proprietary methods for handling and treating the contaminated soil.

At this moment much research on landfarming is carried out in the Netherlands. The University of Amsterdam in co-operation with Heidemij, the Staaring centrum of the Agricultural University of Wageningen and DHV are all investigating the optimization of landfarming from different viewpoints.

DHV has received a grant from the Netherlands Agency for Energy and the Environment in the framework of the Environmental Technology Programme for a further optimization study of the so-called intensive landfarming. This project is carried out in co-operation with the municipality of Amsterdam. The intention is to start a public private partnership for the operation of a factory for intensive landfarming where contaminated soil from the municipality of Amsterdam can be treated. As a first stage of this project, further optimization studies at laboratory and pilot scale will be undertaken. The results of the first pilot studies are given here.

INTENSIVE LANDFARMING

In association with a local contractor DHV started a pilot study to investigate the influence on the landfarm process of several parameters. The project was executed in two phases.

The aim of phase 1 was to clean soil contaminated with mineral oil in three months from approximately 10,000 mg/kg (twice the C level) to 1,000 mg/kg (the B level). After 29 weeks this pilot study was completed, at which time the mineral oil content measured 2,000 mg/kg. During the investigation the rate of degradation decreased. A bioavailability test showed that with an increase in moisture content, enough oil was available for biodegradation. The somewhat disappointing results of this phase probably reflected too low a temperature and, periodically, a moisture content which was too low. The parameters bed height, pretreatment by sieving, tillage and nutrients were not limiting.

The aim of phase 2 was a further cleaning up to B level of the soil remediated in phase 1. The method of soil treatment was further improved for this phase, and in particular the water and air flux was increased, although due to leakage the increase in water flux was not achieved. The aim of phase 2 was achieved: after 19 weeks the mineral oil content of the soil measured approximately 750 mg/kg. There was no further increase of the biodegradation rate. This was probably caused by a low bioavailability (adsorption on the organic matter) and a reduced biodegradability of the oil.

With the improved installation a second soil with a mineral oil concentration of 15,000 mg/kg was also treated in phase 2. Within 19 weeks the mineral oil content decreased to 2,500 mg/kg. The degradation rate in this soil was remarkably high, over 500 mg/kg/d. It should be noted here that the average temperature of the soil bed was also higher.

LANDFARMING OF HARBOUR SLUDGE

On commission from the Institute for Inland Water Management and Waste-water Treatment of the Ministry of Transport, Public Works and Water Management, DHV is investigating the feasibility of landfarming harbour sludge contaminated with mineral oil and PAH. Two different sludges are tested:

- sludge from the Zierikzee harbour (Province of Zeeland) and
- sludge from the Geulhaven (a harbour in the Rotterdam harbour area).

Using these sludges, a laboratory study was started in December 1989. In November 1989 and February 1990 dredged material from the Zierikzee-haven (ZZ) and the Geulhaven (GH) respectively was used in field trials.

After a comprehensive laboratory investigation in November 1989 and February 1990 a pilot field experiment was started. The study involved 10 trial sections. During a period of nine months the trial sections were treated only by tillage. As a result of the laboratory tests it was decided to investigate only four trial sections, two for the ZZ sludge and two for GH sludge. In Table 4.6 the characteristics of the four trial fields are given. The woodchips, compost and sewage sludge were added in July 1991 (week 72 of the experiment).

The preliminary results of the field experiments for the ploughed fields are given in Figure 4.2 overleaf. The results for the non-ploughed fields showed no significant difference from those for the ploughed fields. No results are available yet in respect of the addition of compost, woodchips and sewage sludge, which were added in week 72 after the experiments started.

ADVANTAGES AND LIMITATIONS OF LANDFARMING
On the basis of the results available so far, the advantages of landfarming seem to be the reduction of costs and the recovery and re-use of the contaminated soil. At present the costs charged by firms varies between Dfl 70, and Dfl 100 per ton of polluted sandy soil depending on the degree of pollution. DHV designed a landfarm system for a major oil company in the Rotterdam harbour area, with an annual supply of 5,000–15,000 ton soil polluted with mineral oil products. The estimated costs ranged from Dfl 40 to Dfl 80 per ton. In this situation,

TABLE 4.6
Characteristics of the trial fields for the landfarming of harbour sludge

Sludge	Area (m²)	Height (cm)	Additions
ZZ 1	420	15	Woodchips, compost, sewage sludge
ZZ 2	1250	15	—
GH 1	150	30	Woodchips, compost, sewage sludge
GH 2	150	30	—

71

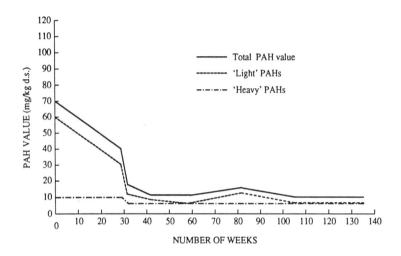

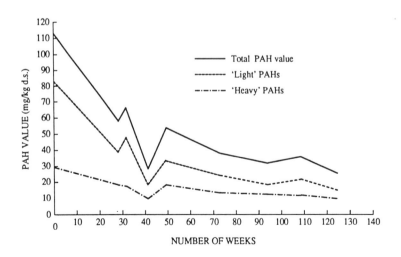

Figure 4.2   Preliminary results of the field experiments for the ploughed fields.

however, the clean-up target was B level (1,000 mg/kg). Normally the soil has to be cleaned up to A level (50 mg/kg).

The strict requirement of meeting A level restricts the applicability of the landfarming technique. It is difficult to predict if, and after what period, this level can be reached. In Figure 4.3 the results of a number of landfarming schemes are summarized and compared with A and B levels.

It is not the limitation of the technique but timescale constraints which determine the feasibility of achieving A level. When the required level can not be reached in a limited period of time, a check on the ecotoxicology of the remaining pollutant concentration might be helpful. At present however the Dutch official policy tends to maintain adherence to an absolute criterion, ie value A, rather than permitting an evaluation of actual remaining risks.

THE FUTURE OF LANDFARMING

As more and more case studies report on the microbial degradation of various hydrocarbon components in various concentrations and in various soil types, kinetic data become increasingly available. These data can be used for further optimization of the technique and for predicting both performance and time period required to meet a specific target. At the same time a greater understanding is gained with respect to ecotoxicological performance which might lead to a more effective design of the technique and a better appreciation of its applicability and its results.

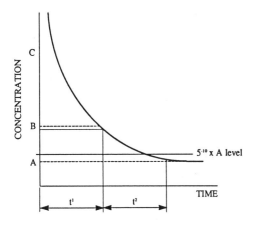

Figure 4.3   Summary of results of several landfarming systems.

DEVELOPMENT OF A BIOREACTOR FOR THE PURIFICATION OF GROUNDWATER

Groundwater encountered in the course of remediation measures will generally have sufficiently high concentrations of contaminating substances to preclude direct discharge into sewage systems or surface waters. Benzene, toluene, ethylbenzene, different isomers of xylene, as well as tetrachloroethene (PCE) and trichloroethene (TCE) are among the compounds, or combinations of compounds, most frequently found in polluted soil and groundwater. These components are usually removed by abstraction of groundwater and purification through physical/chemical methods. The residual products left by such processes unfortunately are still contaminants and thus the environmental problem is not eliminated. Thus, the application of a biological alternative which can destroy or nullify the contamination is desirable.

The development of a biological method of remediation was initiated by DHV in 1986, and aimed at developing a reactor in which, through a biotechnological process, groundwater contaminated by the substances mentioned above could be purified. The strategy followed in this project was threefold:

1.   collation of data on the microbial degradation process of the compounds to be tested;
2.   application of this knowledge in a reactor to be designed and optimized;
3.   customization and testing of the developed reactor concept at a contaminated site.

The fundamental research, which covered microbiological processes, process conditions and optimization of the reactor concept, was conducted by the Microbiology and Environmental Technology Departments of the Agricultural University of Wageningen. DHV Environment & Infrastructure executed the field work, customizing and testing the developed reactor under field conditions.

The project comprised two phases:

Phase A
a1.   implementation of a feasibility study (Schraa et al. 1989(a)[4]);
a2.   laboratory research (Schraa et al. 1989(b)[5]);
a3.   realization of a reactor concept (Schraa et al. 1989(b)[5]).

Phase B
b1.   laboratory research investigating the degradation of aromatics;
b2.   preliminary technological study;

b3. optimization study for a bioreactor;

b4. pilot study for a bioreactor;

b5. investigation of the anaerobic degradation of PCE.

The planning and results of phases b1 to b4 are presented here. The investigation focused on the elimination of volatile mono-aromatics and naphthalene. The description of this investigation and its results is preceded by a summarized explanation of some theoretical aspects of the study. The research concerning anaerobic degradation of tetrachloroethene is published elsewhere (de Bruin et al. 1992(a)[6] and 1992(b)[7]).

THEORETICAL BACKGROUND

A biotechnological process for the elimination of aromatic hydrocarbons from groundwater has to meet three criteria:

1. it must be possible to reach a low concentration of effluent;

2. elimination must be effected mainly through degradation and not through volatilization or adsorption;

3. the mean rate of transformation in the reactor must be high.

Various constituent processes play a role in eliminating aromatic hydrocarbons from groundwater in a three-phase reactor:

• transformation of aromatic hydrocarbons and oxygen in the biofilm;

• transfer of aromatic hydrocarbons from the water phase to the air phase (volatilization);

• transfer of oxygen from the air phase to the water phase;

• adsorption of aromatic hydrocarbons to the biofilm and the carrier material.

Monocyclic aromatic hydrocarbons will adsorb on biomass to a very limited extent, as they have a low octanol-water coefficient. No adsorption processes were thus taken into account during the investigation. The volatilization of aromatic hydrocarbons can be limited by:

1. a low value of the mass transfer coefficient, and the specific interface between air and water;

2. a low absorption capacity of the air flow;

3. the passing of air and water in down-flow through the reactor.

The resistance against substance transfer, for both oxygen and aromatic hydrocarbons, will mainly involve the liquid. Limiting the volatilization of aromatics will automatically result in insufficient aeration, therefore the volatilization should preferably be minimized by limiting the flow rate of the air. The rate of degradation depends on kinetic parameters describing the growth and death of biomass, the thickness of the biofilm and the concentration of biomass in the biofilm. Furthermore, it should be noted that lower substratum concentrations on the biofilm surface will slow down the degradation process, as the intrinsic reaction speed is lowered or the diffusion in the biofilm is limited. In consequence, the mean degradation speed in the reactor can be raised by:

• a large specific surface of the biofilm;

• a high concentration of biomass in the reactor;

• high substratum concentrations at the surface of the biofilm.

The mean concentration of aromatic hydrocarbons can be raised by restricting axial mixing of the water in the reactor. The concentration of oxygen can be raised by ensuring a high aeration capacity. Little experimental data on the conditions required to reach a high biomass concentration per m^2 carrier surface is available, and very little theorizing has taken place so far. The data that is available seems to indicate that the biomass concentration per m^2 carrier surface is proportional to the concentration of the limiting substratum in the water. Sustaining the biofilm needs a certain minimum concentration. Below this minimum the biofilm wears out and dies off at a greater rate than it can grow. In a plug flow reactor this can result in a threshold concentration, a residual concentration which is not degraded.

A 'dry filter' is a packed column with air and water in down-flow through the reactor from the top. Such a filter has several main advantages:

1.   a large specific surface of the carrier material ($1,500–3,000$ m^2/m^3), resulting in a high concentration of biomass;

2.   plug flow features, resulting in high substratum concentrations at the surface of the biofilm;

3.   air and water flow in the same direction through the sand bed, limiting the volatilization of aromatic hydrocarbons;

4.   a high aeration capacity at a low air:water ratio, resulting in a low absorption capacity of the air flow.

OPTIMIZATION INVESTIGATION

The optimization investigation had the following objectives:

1.   investigating the performance of a dry filter in varying processing conditions (hydraulic and organic loads, air:water ratio);

2.   evaluating the stability of the elimination process in a dry filter;

3.   establishing the mutual influence of the various mono-aromatic hydrocarbons on the elimination capacity reached.

76

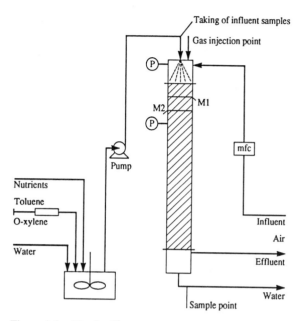

Figure 4.4   The dry filter.

Figure 4.4 is a diagram of the dry filter. Springwater was passed through a closed buffer tank (0.1 m^3) and onto the dry filter, with a Mohno-pump. The xenobiotics and nutrients were added to the stirred contents of the buffer tank. The water was passed down-flow through the dry filter, with a sprinkler ensuring an even distribution across the filter surface. Air was entered simultaneously with the help of a mass flow control unit. The volumes of the reactor and the filterbed amounted to 20.6 and 18.3 litres respectively, their heights to 2.25 m and 1.95 m. Inside the column, sampling points were mounted at various distances in the bed. Above the bed the column was fitted with pressure gauges. The pattern of the pressure drop through the filter bed was monitored constantly. The packing material inside the dry filter consisted of sand (1.5–2.5 mm).

Figure 4.5 overleaf shows the elimination capacity plotted against the influent concentrations of toluene, ortho-xylene and total aromatics, for a hydraulic surface load of 3.8 m^3/m^2/h (water flow = 35 l/h, air flow= 30 l/h).

The dry filter was loaded with both aromatics. Figure 4.5 shows that the elimination capacity of the total aromatics increased in direct proportion to the concentration of influent up to a value of 60 to 70 g/m^3/h. Furthermore, the elimination of aromatics was complete up to this value and with an effluent

77

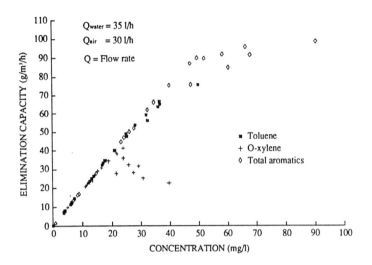

Figure 4.5   Elimination capacity versus influent concentration for toluene, o-xylene and total aromatics with a hydraulic pressure of 3.8 $m^{-2}/m^{-3}/h$.

concentration below 0.5 g/l. When the organic load was increased, the elimination capacity grew to 90 to 100 $g/m^3/h$, but then the aromatics were not totally eliminated, nor did the effluent concentration (100 g/l) meet the standard required for discharge into the sewage system. The elimination capacity of toluene and ortho-xylene was proportionally increased with an increase of influent concentration. The elimination capacity for ortho-xylene reached a maximum of around 40 $g/m^3/h$, after which it started decreasing. The maximum for toluene was double this amount. An explanation for this difference may be found in the fact that the micro-organisms degrading toluene and those degrading ortho-xylene compete for the oxygen.

Figure 4.6 shows the elimination capacity plotted against the total organic load at different hydraulic loads, for which the elimination of aromatics was 100% at an aromatics load of 55 $g/m^3/h$. With regard to the maximum elimination capacity, Figure 4.6 indicates that this capacity showed a slight reduction at increasing hydraulic surface loads with equal aromatics loads.

The optimization investigation also revealed that:

• it was necessary to provide water poor in nitrogen/phosphates with a continuous supply of nutrients in order to reach a high elimination capacity, both during the starting phase and during the continuous-operation phase;

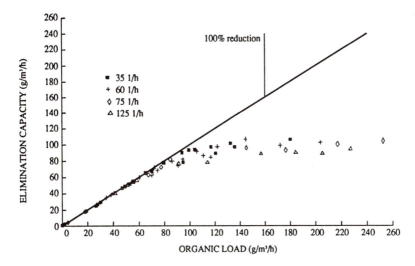

Figure 4.6   Elimination capacity versus organic load at different hydraulic loads.

- the dry filter needed backflushing every three days at an organic load of 50 g/m³/h. Backflushing was done at a pressure drop of 5–8 m water column;

- the elimination of free biomass during backflushing could result in a reduction of the elimination capacity;

- the elimination capacity reached with a mixture of toluene and ortho-xylene corresponded to the elimination capacity reached with a mixture of benzene, toluene, ethylbenzene, and meta-, para- and ortho-xylene;

- the components benzene and ortho-xylene were hardest to eliminate when the filter was overloaded with a BTEX-mixture.

PILOT STUDY WITH A DRY FILTER
After studying the successful elimination of aromatics in a small laboratory-scale dry filter, the performance of a larger reactor was studied under field conditions. Trial runs focused on the standards set in the first phase of the investigation as well as the establishment of the elimination capacity for volatile aromatics and naphthalene. The assessment took the following aspects into consideration:

Management
1. simple;
2. reliable;

3. short starting period;
4. sensitivity with regard to fluctuating loads;
5. frequency of backflushing related to pressure drop.

Elimination capacity
1. elimination capacity concerning volatile aromatics and naphthalene;
2. residual concentrations in effluent;
3. elimination capacity of mixed substances;
4. influence of backflushing behaviour on elimination capacity.

Figure 4.7 shows a schematic representation of the pilot installation, for which the same principles hold as described already. The installation was placed near an operating groundwater purification plant (GPP). Part of the water destined for this GPP was pre-treated and diverted to the pilot installation. The groundwater was dosed with BTEX and naphthalene in a mixing tank, offering the opportunity of increasing the organic load to the values required for the tests. The aromatics were dosed through a pump from a chemicals storage barrel. Table 4.7 shows the dimensions of the dry filter. The sand bed rested on a bottom plate with ducts for the transport of air and water. A backflush blower with a capacity of 40 m³/h and a backflush pump with a capacity of 34 m³/h were installed.

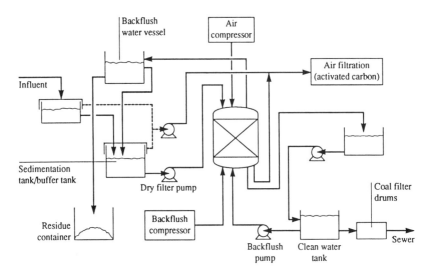

Figure 4.7   Schematic representation of the pilot installation.

During the testing period the hydraulic load was varied from 1.0–2.3 to 3.0–3.4 m^3/h, with the load of aromatics varying from 2 to 25 mg/l.

The testing programme was based on the optimization objectives and was aimed at starting the reactor and establishing the elimination capacity and the backflushing behaviour.

The filter was started in three different ways:

1. by re-circulating the groundwater across the reactor after dosing it with the aromatics;
2. as 1, but after inoculation of the reactor with an enriched culture of micro-organisms;
3. by submerging the reactor in groundwater with aromatics added.

The elimination capacity for aromatics (toluene, ethylbenzene, ortho-xylene and naphthalene) was studied as a function of hydraulic and organic loads. The hydraulic load was varied between 1.0 and 3.4 m^3/h, and the organic load between around 2 and 100 g/m^3/h. During the experimental stage it became clear that a compressor would have to be installed to provide the system with sufficient air. The pilot installation aimed at reaching an effluent concentration for a total of contaminants between 10 and 50 µg/l. The flow rate of air and water, the oxygen content and pH of influent and effluent, and the pressure drop through the filter were monitored daily. Influent and effluent were analysed three times a week for TEX and naphthalene, and occasionally for other parameters.

The reactor was backflushed manually, based on pressure drop. The frequency of backflushing and the influence of this process on the elimination capacity were studied.

The results of the starting experiments could not be unambiguously interpreted. It was concluded, however, that the load of aromatics should be kept small at the start. Both re-circulation and submerging are viable alternatives, both of which should, however, be accompanied by a good oxygen supply.

The elimination capacity may vary widely for each component. Ortho-

TABLE 4.7
Dimensions of the dry filter

Diameter	0.915 m	Volume filterbed	1.0 m^3
Total height	2.9 m	Surface area	0.66 m^2
Height of filterbed	1.5 m	Capacity influent pump	5.0 m^3/h
Total volume of reactor	1.9 m^3	Capacity effluent pump	5.5 m^3/h

xylene generally proved the hardest to eliminate, but with naphthalene 100% elimination could be reached as a rule. Figure 4.8 summarizes the results of the pilot study. The elimination capacity for the total contaminants is presented as a function of the organic load for hydraulic loads between 1.0–2.3 m^3/h and 3.0–3.4 m^3/h. These results lead to the conclusions stated.

An elimination capacity of 100% is feasible for loads up to around 80 g/m^3/h. An adequate oxygen supply is crucial in this respect. When the elimination capacity was significantly lower, this could generally be traced to

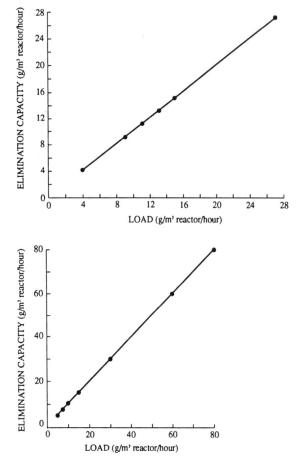

Figure 4.8   Elimination capacity versus organic load (total contaminants) at hydraulic loads of respectively 1.0–2.3 and 3.0–3.4 m^3/h.

an insufficient oxygen supply or problems with the through-flow of the reactor bed. An effluent concentration between 10 and 50 µg/l appears quite feasible, and will allow the effluent of the bioreactor to be discharged directly into the sewage system. From these results it may be concluded that the bioreactor is highly appropriate for the elimination of aromatics from groundwater.

Backflushing of the reactor did not pose any problems provided that the compressor was large enough. The process readily set the sand bed floating, thereby freeing biomass and iron deposits. The organic load also appeared to be an influencing factor. In practice, backflushing was executed every 2 to 3 days on average; increasing this frequency to a daily practice adversely affected the elimination capacity, as it probably inadvertently flushed out biomass as well.

CONCLUSIONS

Based on desk research, laboratory investigations, an optimization study and a pilot study, a bioreactor based on the principle of 'dry filtration' has been developed for the purification of polluted groundwater.

This reactor performs with high organic loads, high elimination capacities (both up to 50–60 g/m^3/h) and low effluent concentrations. The resulting effluent concentrations comply with the standards for discharge to the sewage system. In some cases the effluent concentrations were even lower, suggesting that the reactor system might possibly be used in cases where groundwater is required to be discharged to surface water courses. It is concluded that the system described here is usable for the purification of groundwater contaminated with volatile aromatics. The bioreactor described is technologically and economically competitive with other or comparable techniques.

This project was co-funded by the Netherlands Agency for Energy and the Environment in the framework of the Environmental Technology Programme, the Netherlands Integrated Soil Research Programme and the Institute for Inland Water Management and Waste Water Treatment.

FINALLY

With respect to biological techniques for soil and groundwater remediation, we conclude that:

• biological techniques are still promising and offer advantages compared with physical/chemical techniques;

• the advantages of biological treatment are evident, viz:

— a clean end product is obtained;

— in principle low remaining concentrations of contaminants can be achieved;
— secondary emissions are low;
— by and large (some) cost reductions can be achieved over presently used techniques.

• with actual site results becoming more and more available, further development and optimization of the various techniques should be possible;

• evaluation of feasibility and optimal design are strongly dependent on site specific characteristics;

• biological treatment is technologically and financially a realistic alternative to chemical or physical treatments;

• the standards applied to the evaluation of performance of biological remediation techniques for contaminated land are crucial to the further use of the technology. In terms of concentration (or mass) reduction obtained the techniques are highly effective. However, in terms of resulting absolute concentrations, especially at the low A level applied in the Netherlands, the clean-up target cannot be guaranteed. The strict procedures used in the Netherlands in respect of remediation of contaminated land thus hamper the further development of these techniques.

REFERENCES

1. Keuzenkamp, K.W., Von Meijenfeldt, H.G. and Roels, J.M., 1990, Soil Protection Policy in the Netherlands: the second decade, in *Conf Proc Contaminated Soil '90. Third International KfK/TNO Conference on Contaminated Soil, December 1990. Karlsruhe.* (Vol 1): 3-10.

2. Van Den Hof, J., 1992, Lessons learnt abroad: evaluation the impact of the Dutch register of land which may be contaminated, in *Building your future strategy for the Buying, Selling and Remediation of Contaminated Land, IIR Industrial Conference, London, June 1992.*

3. Franzius, V. and Stietzel, H.J., 1991, The German approach to contaminated land: responsibility, procedure, dimension, technologies, in *Conf Proc Contaminated Land: Policy Regulation and Technology, February 1991, London.*

4. Schraa, G., Bruin de, W., Sluis van, J., Rozema, H., 1989(a), *De ontwikkeling van bioreactoren voor de reiniging van grondwater, Rapportage haalbaarheidsstudie (fase a.1)*, DHV Milieu & Infrastructuur, Amersfoort, Nederland

5. Schraa, G., Bruin de, W., Sluis van, J., Rozema, H., 1989(b), *De ontwikkeling van bioreactoren voor de reiniging van grondwater, Rapportage laboratoriumonderzoek en uitwerking reactorconcept (fase a.2)*, DHV Milieu & Infrastructuur, Amersfoort, Nederland

6. Bruin de, W., Kotterman, J.J., Posthumus, M.A., Schraa, G. and Zehnder, J.B., 1992(a), Complete biological reductive transformation of tetrachloroethane to ethane, *Applied and Environmental Microbiology*, 58 (6): 1996–2000.
7. Bruin de, W. and Schraa G., 1992(b), *Reductieve dechlorering van tetrachlooretheen in een bioreactor*, Landbouwuniversiteit, Wageningen, Nederland.

BIBLIOGRAPHY

Hoek, J.P. van der, *et al.*, 1989, Biological removal of polycyclic aromatic hydrocarbons, benzene, toluene, ethylbenzene, xylene and phenolic compounds from heavily contaminated groundwater and soil, *Environmental Technology Letters* 10: 185–194.

IWACO/de Ruiter Milieutechnologie, 1989, Biologische reiniging van grondwater met behulp van bioreactoren, *DBW-RIZA nota* 89.028 Lelystad, Nederland.

TAUW/DBW-RIZA, 1988, Biologische zuivering van grondwater verontreinigd met HCH's, benzeen en monochloorbenzeen, *DBW-RIZA nota* 88.061, Lelystad, Nederland.

Verheul, J., Doelman, P., 1992, *De ontwikkeling van bioreactoren voor de reiniging van grondwater, Rapportage veldproef*, DHV Milieu & Infrastructuur, Amersfoort, Nederland.

Vis, P., de Bruin, W., Rinzema, A., Schraa, G., 1992, *De ontwikkeling van bioreactoren voor de reiniging van grondwater. Biodegradatie van aromaten: laboratorium en optimalisatieonderzoek*, Landbouwuniversiteit, Wageningen, Nederland

Vlekke, G.J.F.M., Woelders, J.A. and Sillem, J.A., 1989, Biorotor is goed alternatief voor chemische behandeling, *Milieutechniek*, Dec 1989.

5. THE COSTS OF CLEAN-UP
Simon Tillotson

Increased regulatory pressure across Europe and growing concerns over future environmental liabilities mean that landowners are critically examining potential contamination on their sites arising from current or past activities. Industry is becoming aware that in order to reduce short or long-term liability, some form of remediation is required.

THE UK PROBLEM
In the UK, the results of the Department of the Environment survey of derelict land (1988) suggest that up to 27,000 hectares of derelict land could be contaminated. This does not include sites where industrial activity continues. Traditionally, remediation of such sites has involved either the off-site disposal of contaminated materials and/or the encapsulation of materials on site. The current UK government policy on remediation is to encourage clean-up on the back of redevelopment; government grants are based on economic growth potential rather than environmental improvement. Such an approach may overlook the implications of contaminant impact on human health and the natural environment outside areas where development potential is possible.

With an approach which puts the emphasis on redevelopment, the actual cost of clean-up can have a significant impact on the economic viability of the project. At the moment off-site landfilling or on-site encapsulation of contaminants is a relatively cheap option. Other forms of clean-up which focus on the *in situ* treatment of contaminants cannot currently meet the financial constraints set for the redevelopment.

However, the costs of off-site disposal are rising and this encourages waste minimization and clean-up rather than merely storing up environmental problems for the future. Such issues therefore demand effective in situ, on-site or off-site treatment. There is a clear move towards basing clean-up policies on contaminant risk to the environment rather than the development potential of the land.

The factors affecting clean-up in Europe are the following:

- public pressure. It is pressing industry and government for a cleaner environment;

• increasing regulatory pressure. This includes, in the UK context, the enforcement of existing legislation (eg National Rivers Association's powers under the
1991 Water Resources Act) and forthcoming legislation such as the requirement
for a modified Register of Contaminated Land (within the Environmental
Protection Act) and EC directives on groundwater, civil liability and landfills;

• potential environmental liabilities associated with business and property
transactions. These lead to certain operations either not being purchased, or
requiring monies to be set aside or remediation carried out prior to acquisition;

• US-based multi-nationals. Building on experience in the USA, they are
adopting worldwide environmental standards, even in cases where the regulatory framework is not in place. Such policies foresee a future trend towards more
US-style clean-up legislation. To act now is seen both as environmentally
responsible (no double standards between policies in the US and other countries
worldwide) and also as a way to reduce clean-up costs in the long-term;

• economics. There is a growing awareness that clean-up costs are potentially
formidable and must be taken into consideration when asset management is
reviewed and budgets are set.

The introduction of the Contaminative Land Use Registers under
Section 143 of the Environmental Protection Act in the UK may have significant
implications for landowners in terms of property blight, reduction in property
values or adverse investor perceptions. The July 1992 consultation paper on
registers reduced the number of contaminative uses from 42 to 8, so that about
10–15% of the original land area will be included in the register under current
proposals. These include sites which have a high probability of being contaminated, such as gas and coke works, petroleum, chemical manufacturing and
refining plants, manufacture of asbestos or asbestos products, waste disposal
sites, manufacture or refining of lead or steel or an alloy of lead or steel, and
scrapyards. The remaining area will be subject to separate consultation, however, and the form of it is unknown.

A target date for the introduction of the registers has not yet been set
by the DoE. However, the various consultation papers have raised the general
awareness of investors and landowners to the potential liabilities, and increasing
regulatory constraints under the statutory nuisance provisions and the Water
Resources Act. In addition, local political pressures and concerns — particularly
where housing has, or is planned to be, developed on contaminated sites — is a

concern. Furthermore, property institutions and financiers are taking a much more cautious view on sites where contaminative land uses have been identified. Environmental audits are becoming a more standard procedure for property transactions, and in some cases property institutions have pulled out of transactions where there is a high probability that the sites may be included on the register.

The implementation of the European-wide convention on civil liability for environmental damage may also have some implications for the prevention of on-going contamination problems. Under the convention, an operator of a dangerous activity would be liable for damage resulting from incidents at the time when the activity was under his control, including continuous occurrence. In addition, the convention would make provision for cases where damage is discovered only after a dangerous activity has ceased. At this stage it remains to be seen how influential the convention will be on the EC's evolving policy on civil liability for environmental damage which was embodied within a recent draft green paper.

In the USA, the authorities have adopted a litigation-based cost recovery approach to contaminated land issues. This has focused the attention of industry and government on the issue of clean-up and on the need for *in situ* or on-site remediation, and has resulted in the escalation of clean-up costs. It has been estimated recently that, of the costs associated with the federal Superfund sites, 20–40% of all expenditure could be attributed to legal fees resulting from litigation and enforcement issues. With an estimated clean-up bill in excess of $100bn, this represents a staggering amount of money not directly associated with the actual business of cleaning up contamination.

Clearly the 'cook-book' approach to contaminant clean-up in the USA (which results in the requirement in California for groundwater to be cleaned up to below drinking water standards irrespective of the use of the aquifer) and the concept of strict liability (which holds any company or landowner associated with a site responsible for clean-up, irrespective of their actual involvement in the site) have been instrumental in such escalation of the costs.

The message which comes from the US experience can be summarized as follows:

• The costs of clean-up are high. Whilst enforcement provides the driving force for clean-up, the setting of unrealistic (and at times unachievable) goals leads to expensive litigation, delay in clean-up and an escalation in overall costs.

• Potential liabilities associated with any contamination at a site under consideration for acquisition should be carefully assessed throughout the acquisition process. The liability implications of an inaccurate assessment are potentially significant.

• Contaminated sites should be identified and the sites characterized in terms of the nature and extent of contamination and the threat posed by such sites to human health and the environment. The final end-use for a site internally depends on what level of clean-up can be achieved and the risks posed by the site.

• A programme of clean-up based on the actual risk posed by the site to environmental receptors should be adopted, rather than defining non-site specific and potentially unachievable clean-up levels. This can have the effect of reducing overall costs compared with clean-up being based on non-specific standard concentration guidelines.

• Companies should adopt a pro-active approach to clean-up concentrating on prioritizing sites for clean-up in terms of risk and adopting preventative measures to minimize future liabilities. Such an approach can represent cost savings when compared with enforcement or liability actions.

• Properly remediated sites represent a minimizing of environmental and financial liability for a landowner with considerably lower risk to public health and the natural environment both in the short and long term.

As a consequence of the Superfund programme and other legislation, a wide range of clean-up technologies have been developed and field tested at contaminated sites in the United States. Legislation in Europe, particularly in the Netherlands and Germany, has further promoted research on the application of clean-up technologies for contaminated soil and groundwater.

TOWARDS AN INTEGRATED APPROACH

In the UK, the tradition of low cost off-site disposal and the emphasis on redevelopment has lead to a slow take-up in the use of higher technology solutions for clean-up. Whilst a large proportion of the legislation requiring sites to be cleaned up is in place, the push towards a more general requirement for clean-up of existing industrial sites and marginal derelict land awaits enforcement of the legislation.

Despite the research and use of technologies in the USA and Europe, solutions to contamination problems are often unclear. A complication is the availability of competing technologies of varying effectiveness. Selecting an appropriate technology results in considerable savings, avoiding unnecessary cost, delay and pollution from an otherwise only partial clean-up.

This leads to the need for a integrated approach to clean-up. Such an approach characterizes the contaminants in terms of the risk posed to environmental receptors. It also provides a defensible, practical and cost-effective solution, based on a detailed feasibility study of the technologies or combinations of technologies, that can achieve the risk-based clean-up levels defined.

A move away from the 'cook-book' guideline clean-up levels such as the Interdepartmental Committee for the Redevelopment of Contaminated Land (ICRCL) and Dutch ABC levels ensures that a clean-up can be tailored to the site specific conditions encountered.

In basic terms such an approach involves the following steps:

• Preliminary assessment — determination of potential presence of contamination and liability associated;

• Focused investigation — characterization of nature and extent of contamination;

• Risk assessment — determination of clean-up levels based on risks posed by the contamination to human health and environment;

• Feasibility studies — detailed assessment of relative cost effectiveness, implementability and practicability of options;

• Implementation;

• Verification and aftercare — including provision of management document to regulate future development on site, as appropriate.

DEFINING THE CONTAMINATION PROBLEM

The need to define the nature and extent of any contamination at sites with suspected contaminated land arises from the need to assess the potential environmental liability of the site under consideration. This potential liability ranges from on-site worker health and safety, to the control of effluent emissions and clean-up of contaminated soil and groundwater. Each site has a different set of current and historical operating characteristics and local environmental setting. The approach of the investigation must therefore be tailored to the unique characteristics of each site and must be moved forward in an integrated, phased manner.

The development of an appropriate clean-up strategy depends upon a properly planned and executed investigation of environmental conditions at the site. Environmental audits (whether part of a pre-acquisition investigation or as an assessment of environmental performance) or knowledge of spills or other environmental incidents can often indicate the potential existence of contamination. To characterize the nature and extent of suspected contamination, a site investigation is required. Such investigations should focus on:

- the nature of the facility or property under consideration including a review of site history, location of chemical storage areas, underground tanks, etc and current site conditions;

- the details of the proposed development (if redevelopment is proposed);

- as complete a characterization of the nature and extent of contamination as possible;

- an evaluation of the environmental context of the observed contamination;

- definition of geological and hydrogeological setting.

Such assessments, when related to pre-acquisition transactions, are typically undertaken on tight schedules, and the scope of the investigation needs to be focused. Therefore, pre-acquisition assessments generally concentrate on areas of a site where the potential for significant contamination is greatest, and samples collected from these areas are analysed in the laboratory for a broad range of parameters. Such investigations rely on the findings of the audit inspection. The data gaps from such assessments may have to be filled with follow-up site investigations in order to develop a coherent clean-up strategy. Additionally, for investigations where timescales are less strict, the actual conditions encountered may require more focused investigations to be carried out to enable clean-up strategies to be developed.

The general approach to conducting site investigations at sites where there is expected to be some form of clean-up is reviewed below.

AUDIT ASSESSMENT TO DEFINE THE POTENTIAL FOR CONTAMINATION
The amount of information available on the site history depends to a large extent upon the current use of the site and, in particular, whether the site is an operational facility or derelict.

As much information as possible should be collected about the nature of the past and current manufacturing operations at the site, the types of chemicals used at the facility, waste disposal practices, chemical spills or other environmental accidents and related information which may give an indication of the types of contaminants at the site. In addition, a preliminary site survey of any operating facility should be carried out. This survey should encompass a thorough tour of the facility, including inspection of chemical storage areas, underground tankage, any waste disposal areas and a review of available records on the compliance with any discharge permits, environmental incidents such as spills and historical operations at the site.

The preliminary site survey should focus on past and current raw material storage, product and waste storage and handling practices which present the potential for releases of contaminants to the environment. These include such practices as storage in below-ground or non-bunded above-ground tanks, conveyance of potentially contaminating materials in below-ground piping, on-site disposal of wastes and evidence of poor housekeeping. Visual evidence of potential contamination should also be considered. Additionally, the preliminary audit should review published documentation on the local and regional geology and hydrogeology. Such an assessment provides an indication of the potential for contaminant migration from the site, in particular:

- the nature of the geology underlying the site and in particular the potential for migration of contaminants from the property
- the presence of and depth to groundwater
- the use of the aquifer for potable or other supply
- the groundwater flow direction and potential exposure routes for contaminants reaching the groundwater.

FIELD INVESTIGATIONS TO CHARACTERIZE THE NATURE AND EXTENT OF CONTAMINATION

Information collected from the review of site history and current operating procedures is used to develop an approach to the field sampling and analytical component of the investigation. The objective of this effort is to identify the specific contaminants present at the site and to gain an understanding of the vertical and lateral extent of the observed contamination. Typically, field investigations carried out in this phase for soil and groundwater contamination assessment can be summarized as follows:

Soil

As a result of the review of the site history and current operating procedures, areas with the potential for soil contamination will be identified. This soil contamination can be addressed by conducting a staged investigation of the apparent source area of the contamination. The initial phase of investigation commonly employs field screening methods to delineate the approximate area and general magnitude of the problem. This is typically followed by a focused soil sampling and analysis effort designed to confirm the results of the initial screening.

Trial pitting using a back-hoe excavator is probably the most common technique for investigating the condition of shallow sub-surface soil. Visual evidence of contamination (staining, landfilled material, etc) as well as odours can be used to select locations of samples for laboratory analysis. Areas of apparent soil contamination exposed through trial pitting would include areas with both inorganic (metals mainly) and organic (solvents, petrol, etc) contaminants. Trial pitting over a relatively small site (1–3 acres) can generally be accomplished in one to two days.

Soil gas surveys can also be used for evaluating a large area in a relatively short period of time. Soil gas surveys measure the total concentration of volatile organic compounds (VOCs) in soil, and are therefore useful for identifying areas with organic contamination (petrol, solvents, etc). The method involves advancing a number of soil borings (by hand or using a drilling rig) in the area of interest and then using a field organic vapour analyser (OVA) to measure the soil gas in the borings. Alternatively, an on-site mobile laboratory such as a field gas chromatograph (GC) can be used to identify selected organic compounds. However, use of a field GC can add substantially to the cost of a soil gas survey. The time to complete a soil gas survey ranges from a day to a week or more, depending upon the nature of the source area, the size and complexity of the site and the soil conditions at the site.

Soil gas surveys are particularly useful in the vicinity of an above-ground or below-ground tank which is suspected to be leaking or in an area where some other form of release of petrol or organic solvent is suspected. Because the soil gas survey normally measures total VOCs and is conducted under varying field conditions (eg barometric pressure, temperature), the results are generally relied upon as an initial screening tool only. Soil gas surveys delineate the apparent extent of soil contamination and identify locations for the collection of samples for more rigorous analysis conducted in a laboratory.

Soil samples for laboratory analysis are collected using hand-held equipment or by advancing soil borings using a drilling rig. These samples are then submitted to a laboratory for analysis of a preselected list of constituents, which is based upon the nature of the source area (determined in the preliminary site inspection). Soil samples should be collected not only from within apparent source areas, but also at the suspected margins of the source areas in an effort to calculate the vertical and lateral extent of soil contamination.

Evidence of soil contamination in deeper borings that approach the water table suggest that groundwater is likely to be contaminated beneath and down gradient from the contaminant source area. The volume of the release and the hydrogeological conditions are key factors in determining whether groundwater beneath the release is contaminated.

Groundwater

The investigation of hydrogeological conditions at the site involves not only the evaluation of groundwater quality but also a range of other data pertaining to groundwater flow directions, thicknesses and positions of aquifers and confining units and potential discharges for groundwater such as local abstraction wells or surface water bodies. This information is essential to the understanding of potential exposure routes for contaminants in groundwater, particularly in areas where groundwater is a significant supply of drinking water.

The investigation of groundwater at the site typically involves a review of available published information on both the local hydrogeological setting and local water abstractions. In addition, any well logs for on-site abstraction wells or groundwater monitoring wells are reviewed to provide site-specific data. From these data and from the data collected earlier in the investigation, locations for groundwater monitoring wells are selected.

The installation of groundwater monitoring wells must be responsive to the local geological conditions and should follow rigorous procedures for the decontamination of drilling equipment and well construction materials. The locations of the monitoring wells in relation to the potential on-site contaminant source areas and potential off-site receptors is critical. A minimum of three wells is necessary in order to determine the direction of groundwater flow at the site. Typically, one well is installed at the up gradient boundary of the site and at least two wells are positioned at locations down gradient from suspected source areas. Additional wells, located at the down gradient site boundary, may be necessary to determine whether contaminated groundwater is flowing off site.

Not only are the locations of the wells important, but the well construction specifications are also critical and should be designed by a qualified hydrogeologist. Improperly designed and installed monitoring wells can lead to further contamination of groundwater, particularly in complex hydrogeological settings.

Once the groundwater monitoring wells are installed, groundwater samples are taken and are submitted to a laboratory for analysis. As for soil samples, the parameters analysed for groundwater are determined based upon a review of the potential contaminants at the site. Additional hydrogeological testing may follow the collection of groundwater samples and may include the following:

• measurement of water levels in on-site and off-site groundwater monitoring wells and surface water bodies to determine vertical and horizontal groundwater flow directions;

• pump testing of selected wells to estimate the yield of the aquifer and a variety of other quantitative hydrogeological parameters;

• continuous water level monitoring of selected wells to measure the effects of off-site abstraction or tidal influences on groundwater beneath the site.

The amount of time necessary to complete the field portion of a hydrogeological investigation varies widely with the hydrogeological conditions at the site and with the number of monitoring wells needed to adequately characterize it. Drilling and sampling the minimum three wells can normally be accomplished in as few as five days at sites where the water table is shallow.

EVALUATION OF THE ENVIRONMENTAL CONTEXT OF THE OBSERVED CONTAMINATION

The significance of the observed contamination can only be assessed in the context of the local environmental setting. The mobility of the contaminants, the location of on-site and off-site human and environmental receptors, the size and shape of the groundwater plume, the presence of free product on the water table, background concentrations and intended use of the site are all factors that are considered in assessing the significance of the contamination. These factors can be integrated by developing a conceptual model for the site, showing the inter-relationship between source locations, transport media (groundwater, surface water, vapours, etc) and potential exposure points.

For example, a leak in an underground storage tank has, over time, caused significant soil and groundwater contamination beneath the manufacturing facility. Directly beneath the tank, soil in the unsaturated zone has been contaminated as the 'product' (in this case petrol or solvent) migrated downward to the water table. A pool of 'free product', commonly referred to as 'non-aqueous phase liquid' (NAPL), floats on the water table and provides a continuing source of 'dissolved phase' contamination to the groundwater. In addition, vapours from the dissolved groundwater contamination and the free product cause further soil contamination in the unsaturated overburden.

In this hypothetical example, the key environmental concerns, or liabilities, which require consideration in the development of a clean-up strategy include the following:

- the contaminated soil in the unsaturated zone directly beneath the tank represents a continuing source of groundwater contamination through infiltration of rainwater;
- the free product floating on the water table has the potential for extending the contamination over a wider area through release of vapours and represents a significant source of groundwater contamination through dissolution;
- soil and groundwater contamination beneath the site may give off vapours that adversely affect worker health and safety;
- contaminated groundwater over a wide area has led to contamination of the deeper fractured bedrock aquifer as well as a river which is at the down gradient, western margin of the site;
- the concentrations of contaminants in the river may be sufficiently high to cause environmental degradation of aquatic and terrestrial habitats in the area;
- uptake of contaminants by fish and other organisms in the river may result in the contaminants being concentrated in their tissue and may affect the health of other wildlife or humans who eat the fish;
- the potable groundwater abstraction well, although shown to be unaffected by the contamination, could be affected in time as either the groundwater contaminant plume spreads further laterally or as the rate of groundwater abstraction increases (eg during a prolonged drought);
- other potable groundwater or surface water abstraction points in the area could be affected, including wells completed in the deeper fractured bedrock aquifer.

A clean-up strategy would have to be developed adequately to control the risks to human health and the environment posed by this hypothetical site.

DEFINITION OF CLEAN-UP LEVELS

Currently, clean-up levels adopted for remediation are based upon either trigger levels contained within guidance notes prepared by government advisory bodies (eg ICRCL and Dutch ABC guidelines) or on Standards, such as US drinking water standards. The disadvantages of using such standard, fixed levels for all sites are:

- such guidelines are not site specific, which can have a significant impact on costs. For example, in California clean-up levels for groundwater contamination have been set below US drinking water standards, irrespective of whether the aquifer is used for potable or any other supply purpose and irrespective of whether such levels can be obtained;

• the guidelines, such as ICRCL and Dutch ABC levels, were not specifically designed for clean-up. Rather, they were developed to provide an indication of the degree of contamination encountered in site investigations;

• the guidelines are incomplete, both in terms of contaminants listed and in the case of the UK ICRCL guidance note, levels for concentrations in groundwater;

• the guidelines are non-statutory.

A site cleaned up to such levels at the current time could be regarded as still contaminated in the future, if new guidelines or tighter clean-up levels become statutory. Such an approach does not provide a landowner with a defensible rationale for clean-up when viewed from the future.

An alternative approach, and one which is increasingly gaining favour in the United States, is the development of risk-based clean-up levels. Such an approach is based upon assessing the contamination present in terms of the risk posed to human health and the natural environment based upon site-specific exposure assessment. Exposure pathways to potential receptors are developed based on the site-specific conditions, the end-use options being considered and the toxicity of individual chemicals which pose the most significant concern. The risk posed to selected receptors is then determined and the clean-up levels defined in terms of an acceptable risk level. In terms of acceptable risk levels, target levels for carcinogens are normally defined in the range 1 in 10,000 to 1 in a million. Target levels are therefore quantified as thresholds which protect human health.

The advantages of this approach are:

• the clean-up levels defined are based on site-specific data and conditions, which has a clear implication for cost of clean-up;

• the levels are specific to the proposed end-use or are set to ensure that a range of end-uses can be achieved without unacceptable risk to future end-users;

• it provides a comprehensive assessment of parameters of concern identified in the site investigation;

• the levels defined are sensitive to human health and environmental impacts;

• the levels are less sensitive to statutory change;

• the rationale behind clean-up to specific levels is defensible. This is especially important in the light of increasingly tight regulatory controls and the potential need for companies to justify clean-ups in the future.

CLEAN-UP OPTIONS

In this section, a number of clean-up options are summarized for soil and groundwater contamination. The discussion begins with relatively straightforward options for soil contamination (ie excavation and removal, capping) and proceeds by reviewing increasingly sophisticated clean-up options for soil and groundwater contamination. The applicability of the clean-up options discussed here depends to a large extent upon the following:

• the risk to human health and the environment posed by the observed contamination;

• the amount of financial resources available to apply to the clean-up of the site;

• the nature of the use/proposed redevelopment of the site;

It is important to emphasize that, with the exception of simple single substance contamination such as refined oil product spills, the remediation is unlikely to be achieved by a single technology. The complex mix of contaminants which usually represents a contamination problem requires the application of a combination of techniques. The development of a cost-effective and implementable clean-up strategy depends upon:

• the nature and extent of contamination present at the site, especially the spread of contamination beyond the site boundary and the extent of groundwater contamination;

• the risks posed by the contaminants to human health and the natural environment;

• the range of remedial technologies available;

• the cost effectiveness, implementability, practicality and timescale for remedial alternatives;

• the implications of a particular clean-up strategy on the surrounding area in terms of worker and public health and the environmental soundness of the technologies.

The following section reviews a number of the wide range of clean-up options available for site remediation and defines typical costs.

CLEAN-UP OPTIONS FOR SOIL

Institutional controls

One of the simplest, and potentially least expensive, measures for eliminating access to contaminated soil is to implement one or more so-called institutional controls. Institutional controls are not clean-up options *per se*, but are measures designed to limit contact with contaminated soil. Examples of institutional controls include erection of fencing around the perimeter of the area of concern to restrict access and the development of zoning/planning restrictions for the site, designed to limit future land use.

The use of fencing and/or restrictions on landuse has the positive effects of protecting human health and the environment, even though the contaminated soil would remain on site. In time, natural attenuation can actually reduce the concentrations of some forms of contamination to some degree, thereby reducing the risk associated with exposure to the soil. However, some degree of trespass may be expected to occur and exposure to contamination lying on the surface may not be eliminated entirely.

Institutional controls have limited application, in particular they:

• leave the source of soil contamination in place which may have the undesired effect of causing further contamination of other media (eg groundwater, surface water, air);

• restrict landuse options which may limit the design or scope of a proposed redevelopment scheme;

• cause housing blight of surrounding residential properties, where house prices are adversely affected by the public knowledge of such soil contamination;

• limit the amount of land available for any development, especially in a crowded industrial estate. Such loss of land may be considered unacceptable.

It would seem that institutional controls are best suited for soil contamination that occupies a relatively small area in a site which is not limited by available land for development. Moreover, this option is best suited for soil contaminated by relatively non-toxic and immobile constituents (eg selected metals and polynuclear aromatic hydrocarbons). The costs to implement this remedy for soil contamination would be low and generally restricted to the costs of installing fencing and securing appropriate deed and/or landuse restrictions.

Capping

One of the more commonly applied measures for dealing with soil (and groundwater) contamination is capping of contaminant source areas. A number of cap designs may be considered depending on the availability and cost of cover materials, the nature of the wastes being covered, the desired performance of the cap and the projected future uses of the site. Capping is intended to achieve two objectives. First, to minimize the amount of precipitation that infiltrates into contaminated soil, thereby reducing the amount of dissolved contamination reaching the water table, and second, to prevent direct contact with contaminated soil by humans or wildlife.

The capping material may be as simple as gravel, clay, asphalt or concrete in the case of a single-layer cap. More complex caps may include an upper layer of vegetated topsoil, underlain by a drainage layer (sand or gravel) over a low permeability layer (consisting of a combined synthetic membrane and clay liner system).

Prior to cap installation, the soil at the site is typically compacted and graded to direct run-off to catchments; following cap installation, the site can either be landscaped and revegetated to prevent erosion or it can be prepared for construction of buildings.

Capping is a proven and reliable technology for isolating contaminants from the above-ground environment, providing significant reductions in contaminated migration via infiltration of water. A properly designed clay cap alone can reduce the vertical permeability of an area to 1.0×10^{-7} cm/s; multilayer caps can achieve even lower permeabilities.

The final cap requires inspection regularly for signs of erosion, settlement or subsidence. In addition, the vegetation on the cap should be maintained by mowing to prevent perforation of the cap liner by deep rooting plants and burrowing animals. The useful life of a properly-designed cap can range from 20 to 60 years or longer. However, the operational lifetime is finite and constraints have to be applied to ensure the integrity of the capping system. The costs for capping would be expected to be in the range of 20–60/m^2, depending upon the cap specifications and the site layout.

Excavation and removal

Another commonly applied technology for contaminated soil is the physical excavation and removal of source material for treatment or disposal on or off site. Excavation is generally accomplished with heavy construction equipment, such as JCBs, bulldozers and loaders. The more conventional options for the treatment or disposal of excavated soil include incineration and off-site disposal in a landfill.

Incineration is a very effective treatment technique which permanently and completely destroys organic contaminants in soil. The incineration can take place at either a licensed facility off site or, less commonly, on site through use of a mobile incinerator. Wastes from the incineration process are relatively inert and consist of solids and non-volatile materials discharged as ash and volatile constituents and some carry-over solids (eg fly ash) vented to the atmosphere with the exhaust gas. Although the ash from the incineration process would be considered non-hazardous for the purpose of disposal, exhaust gases require treatment prior to release.

Off-site disposal involves transporting excavated materials from the site to a licensed disposal facility (landfill). The nature of the constituents in the excavated material determines whether disposal at a hazardous waste landfill is required. This activity may have to be conducted in conjunction with the importation of clean fill material to permit restoration of the site to its original grade. The costs to dispose of contaminated soil in a licensed disposal landfill would be expected to be in the range of £35–75/m³.

Although excavation and removal of contaminated soil achieves the key objective of eliminating the source of soil contamination from the site, accomplishing this objective can actually increase the risk of exposure to contaminated soil. Adverse impacts to human health and the environment can occur during excavation, processing and transportation of the soil. In some cases, the risk of excavation and removal may actually be higher than leaving the soil in place. Moreover, the costs for off-site incineration especially are formidable and are generally in the range of at least £100–400/m³.

Stabilization/solidification
The stabilization/solidification process involves the mixing of cementatious material (similar to Portland cement) or pozzolanic reagents (such as fly ash) to the contaminated soil with the intent of creating a chemically inert and structurally sound matrix. The process can take place at the site either *in situ* (requiring no excavation) or above ground in a defined area. The additives assist in chemically binding both inorganic and organic contaminants in a final matrix, which typically shows unconfined compressive strengths similar to a soil-cement mix.

Although the contaminants remain at the site, they are physically bound in a stabilized mass that limits the risk of exposure. One of the primary drawbacks of the treatment technique relates to increased risks of impacts to human health and the environment during excavation and handling of soil contaminated with VOCs. This risk can be mitigated by using sound construction practices and by containing and treating air emissions during excavation. Costs to carry out this clean-up method would be in the range of £10–50/m³.

Low temperature thermal stripping

Low temperature thermal stripping is typically accomplished by physically disturbing the soil then applying sufficient heat to the soil to drive off volatile and selected semi-volatile organic contaminants. The organic-laden gas from the process can be treated by some form of emissions control (eg fume incinerator) or may be discharged directly to the atmosphere if no treatment is required to meet emissions standards. This method is most effective at relatively shallow depths that do not exceed the limits of excavation equipment (eg 5–10 m).

Costs for this treatment technique are in the range of £50–120/m^3. However, these costs increase as a fume incinerator or other emission controls are added to the process; although the achieved reduction in air emissions significantly reduces the risk of exposure to contaminants.

Biological treatment

Biological treatment techniques utilize bacteria to degrade organic pollutants. There are two main forms of biotreatment: in bio-stimulation bacteria in the soil are stimulated by the introduction of nutrients to the soil enhancing the biodegradation. In bio-augmentation bacteria are formulated and added to the soils on site.

Two techniques used in bioremediation are aqueous biological treatment and landfarming.

Aqueous biological treatment is used for the remediation of liquids, slurries and solids. The wastes are typically placed in a tank with water. The contents are vigorously mixed and aerated in order to supply contact between the microbes and the organic matter, and to provide oxygen so that the biological reaction can take place. Recently, equipment has been adapted from the mining industry so that solids and heavy sludges can be placed in reactors and kept in suspension with relatively high suspended solids concentrations. Since the detention time in a biological system may be from one day to several weeks, by keeping the solids concentration in the mixed reactor high, minimization of the tank size or alternatively an increase in the throughput capacity of the treatment system is possible.

A number of industries have for many years been treating organic sludges or solids by technology referred to as landfarming. Using this technology, the organic waste is applied to the surface of a suitable tract of land. The waste is then mixed into the top 20–30 cm of soil using agricultural or construction equipment. The tilling provides oxygen to the naturally occurring microbes which then degrade the organics. Again nutrients, in the form of fertilizer, are added and the pH adjusted as necessary.

The costs for biological treatment can range between £20–60/tonne. However, there are several advantages and disadvantages in using the bioremediation process. It can be used to treat hydrocarbons and certain other organic compounds, particularly water soluble pollutants. It is environmentally sound since *in situ* bioremedation does not usually generate waste products. It utilizes indigenous microbes and the process is generally economical.

The disadvantages of *in situ* bioremediation are that microbes can be inhibited by heavy metals and some organics, that bacteria can plug or foul the soil and reduce circulation and that introduction of nutrients could adversely affect nearby surface waters. In addition residues may cause taste and odour problems, labour and maintenance requirements could be high and long-term effects are unknown.

Vacuum extraction

In situ vacuum extraction, also commonly known as soil vacuuming, can be an extremely effective clean-up technique for unsaturated soil contaminated with volatile and selected semi-volatile organic compounds. The system consists of a network of air withdrawal (or vacuum) wells installed throughout the area of contaminated soil. The wells are connected to a vacuum pump system which provides continuous air flow through the soil.

The withdrawn air is directed through a treatment system to remove the organic contaminants prior to release to the atmosphere. Examples of treatment systems include a column of granular activated carbon (GAC) or a fume incinerator. The organic contaminants adsorbed onto the GAC are periodically stripped from the carbon and taken off site for reuse or incineration; the fume incinerator destroys the organic contaminants altogether.

In some systems, injection wells are used at the perimeter of the contaminated zone to increase airflow through the soil and to aid in contaminant stripping. In addition, some form of nearly impervious surface cover is commonly used to ensure that airflow pathways are nearly horizontal. Figure 5.1 is a schematic diagram of a vacuum extraction system. Costs to clean up soil using a system similar to the vacuum system shown in Figure 5.1 would be approximately £10–65/m^3.

In situ vitrification

In-situ vitrification (ISV) uses electricity to literally melt inorganic materials into a glass-like inert product. Electrodes are placed into the ground in a

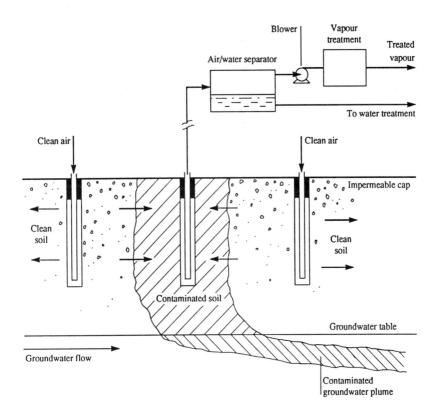

Figure 5.1   Schematic of a soil vapour extraction system.

box-shaped pattern. A starter path of flaked graphite and glass frit is placed at the surface between electrodes. As current is applied, the molten path at a temperature of 1600°C moves down at 25–30 mm/h. The once molten material takes on the characteristics of obsidian after it has cooled. Volume reductions of 20–40% have been achieved.

ISV works primarily on solids such as soil and sand. It will not work on water or oily sludge. Besides *in situ* applications, ISV can be used in various other applications:

• staged — where waste is placed for treatment;
• barrier wall — partial treatment plus containment;
• in-container from high-volume reduction materials;
• stacked settings for very deep treatment.

105

One ISV unit can treat 100–120 tonnes of waste per day. Organics are destroyed by being broken down into their atomic constituents by the intense heat, a process known as pyrolysis. Organics have been destroyed at levels of 89.0 to 99.9999% for an overall destruction and removal efficiency which includes the off-gas treatment. However, one recent test in the USA has shown that 20% of trichlorobenzene had migrated from the melted mass into surrounding soil. This led to a question of the efficacy of ISV and is now being reviewed by a sub-committee of the US House Energy and Commerce Committee.

Volatile contaminants driven off as gases are collected by a negative vent hood placed over the area being treated. The gases are then routed through a treatment system where they are cooled, scrubbed, filtered and chemically treated before release.

The presence of groundwater and buried metals can influence the efficiency of the power supply. Steps can be taken to drain down the water table or install underground barriers. Excess metals can result in a short circuit.

The costs of this technique are reported at £150–300/tonne. Questions about this relatively unproven technology relate to its effectiveness, the requirement for larger amounts of technical investment and a high electrical input (750 kWh per tonne).

CLEAN-UP OPTIONS FOR GROUNDWATER
Many of the clean-up technologies already discussed for soil have the effect of limiting further contamination of groundwater through reduced infiltration (capping), reduced mobility of contaminants (stabilization/solidification), physical removal of the source area (excavation and removal) or treatment of the contaminants in the source area (low temperature thermal stripping and *in situ* vacuum extraction). However, none of these techniques has the ability to remove dissolved contamination in groundwater. The two most practical options for the clean up of contaminated groundwater include multi-well groundwater pump and treat systems and single-well point-of-use treatment systems. These clean-up options are briefly reviewed below.

Groundwater pump and treat systems
Groundwater contaminated with organic and, less commonly, inorganic constituents present in the dissolved phase is most effectively cleaned up in the vicinity of the contaminant source area through installation of a multi-well pump and treat system. In this clean-up option, a series of groundwater recovery wells is

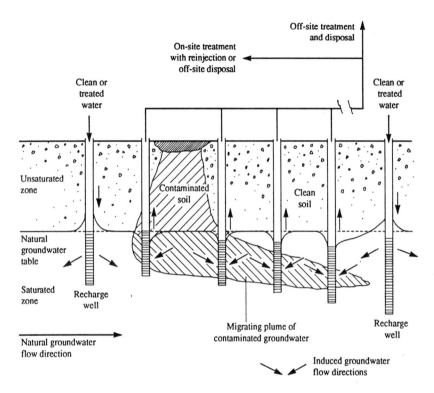

Figure 5.2   Schematic of a contaminated groundwater abstraction system.

installed at strategic locations within the groundwater contaminant plume. Groundwater is abstracted from the wells continuously and directed to an above-ground treatment system, designed to remove the contaminants from the water. Over time, the spread of contaminants in groundwater is contained, and the contaminant plume is slowly recovered and treated. Figure 5.2 schematically depicts the clean-up of a groundwater contaminant plume using a multi-well pump and treat system.

A wide range of above-ground treatment systems exists for recovered groundwater, depending upon the particular nature of contaminants present. A relatively simple spray irrigation system in which VOCs are allowed to volatilize directly to the atmosphere may be appropriate. The nature of contaminants at other sites may require that a complex air stripper, bioremediation (see Figure 5.3 overleaf) or other system be designed to treat groundwater.

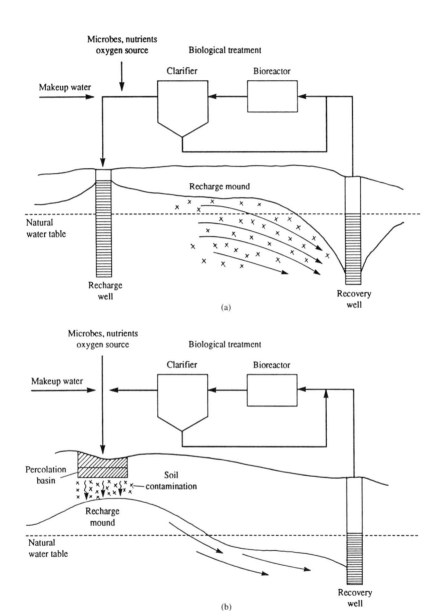

Figure 5.3   Schematic of typical bioremediation systems: (a) using active recharge of recovery; (b) using passive recharge of recovery.

In some pump and treat systems, the treated groundwater is reinjected into the aquifer to enhance recovery of the plume. In other systems, discharge permits to surface water bodies must be obtained; these can be especially difficult to obtain, as the discharge of treated groundwater at many larger sites is in the order of 200–500 gallons/minute. Clearly, 'disposal' of treated water is a key issue for these systems.

Combinations of pump and treat and vacuum extraction are relatively common in the USA, where dual purpose wells are constructed. The injection of air (sometimes heated) results in the increased volatilization of compounds which are then captured by the vapour extraction system. The effectiveness of vapour removal is enhanced by the groundwater drawdown achieved by water pumping.

Two aspects of groundwater pump and treat systems are particularly striking and require further comment. These are the timescale to realize the clean-up objectives for groundwater, and the initial operational and maintenance (O&M) costs for the systems.

Under the US Superfund programme, where admittedly the clean-up objectives are particularly (and arguably unrealistically) stringent, the estimated time to achieve these clean-up objectives is typically measured in decades. The most commonly quoted timeframe is 30 years, and the objective of the pump and treat effort is to restore the aquifer to near-pristine conditions.

There is a growing feeling among scientists involved in these clean-up programmes that meeting these clean-up objectives is technically unachievable, even with an extended timeframe for the pump and treat systems (Travis and Doty, 1990)[4]. A potentially more realistic set of clean-up objectives would still require a system operating continuously for a number of years, perhaps a decade or more. Moreover, the system may merely contain the off-site migration of the plume and reduce the overall mass of contaminants in groundwater, thereby falling short of making the groundwater potable again. Clearly a law of diminishing returns exists when attempting to clean-up to extremely low contaminant levels. In such case, the on-going limitation of off-site migration of contaminants becomes a key issue, along with the action of risks posed by the site being cleaned up to a less stringent level. A situation may arise where, for the expenditure of many thousands of pounds, no significant extra risk elevation occurs.

Constructing and continuously operating a groundwater pump and treat system for even a few years is a formidable task both technically and financially. Typical initial construction costs for recovery well installation and treatment system can exceed £150,000, while annual operation and maintenance costs are generally in the vicinity of £100,000. Clearly, these are the sorts of costs that can significantly impact the economics of an acquisition, potentially rendering the actual value of the property less than the cost of clean-up. In addition, the construction and operation of the pump and treat system may interrupt the schedule for the acquisition and proposed use of the site, particularly if new construction is planned for the acquired property.

Point-of-use treatment systems

Point-of-use treatment systems are small-scale systems designed for installation at the location of abstraction wells which pump groundwater affected by dissolved contamination. These systems are typically designed to remove the contaminants from the water prior to its use as a potable water supply or as a supply of water for livestock or irrigation. Point-of-use treatment systems may be used in conjunction with a multi-well pump and treat system to address the unrecoverable portion of the plume which has left the site boundary.

Costs for point-of-use systems are certainly more reasonable than for multi-well pump and treat systems (generally £1000–2000/household). However, these systems have to be monitored regularly and often require delicate negotiations with local residents, the press, local water companies and the appropriate regulatory authorities. Nevertheless, point-of-use systems are a necessary component in the clean-up of groundwater that is contaminated with potentially harmful constituents.

SUMMARY AND CONCLUSIONS

The conclusions that arise from this assessment of clean-up strategies are as follows:

• increasing public pressure on government and industry for a cleaner environment is playing a key role in the requirement to clean up contaminated soil, groundwater and other media at sites in the UK and elsewhere within the EEC;

• potential liabilities associated with any contamination at a site under consideration for an acquisition should be carefully assessed in a thorough preacquisition environmental audit and investigation;

• development of a coherent clean-up strategy for soil and groundwater contamination in particular depends upon a well-planned site investigation, tailored to the specific environmental conditions at the site. Inadequate investigation can lead to inappropriate or inadequate clean-up solution which can leave the site only partially cleaned up for a cost significantly greater than that for an alternative clean-up option;

• a wide range of technologies exists for the clean-up of contaminated soil and groundwater; many of the more complex technologies have been field tested and proven under the US Superfund programme;

• The implementation of soil and groundwater clean-up efforts can have a significant impact on the economics of any acquisition or redevelopment and on the proposed use of the acquired property or business;

• significant cost savings can be achieved by the use of site-specific risk-based clean-up levels as opposed to the use of non-site specific trigger level concentrations;

• risk-based clean-up levels enable companies to defend clean-ups to future regulators. The use of non-site specific guidelines cannot accomplish this;

• the introduction of the contaminative land use registers under Section 143 of the Environmental Protection Act 1990 will raise public concerns over specific areas of land. The assessment of land by landowners to determine if contamination is present will become a requirement. Investigations to characterize such contamination and prioritize clean-up on risk-based criteria are likely to be needed to avoid planning blight, to assess the final implication of such contamination and to satisfy the regulatory authorities that no risk is posed by the site. Such work will have the dual purpose of showing environmental responsibility and reducing potential financial liabilities. The cost implications of carrying out such asset management at an early date could be significant;

• no single clean-up technology is likely to provide the required solution. It is important given the wide range of contaminants at most sites to carry out a thorough feasibility assessment of remedial options prior to the choice of solution. A combination of solutions is likely. A cost benefit analysis combined with an assessment of the implementability and practicality of the options is required. Only by an integrated approach to such assessments can clean-up be certain of achieving a cost-effective status.

REFERENCES

1. Diehl, D.S., *Waste Treatment Technology Development*, ERM South-west Inc.
2. Parr, M.S., Simonson, J.C.B. and Morin, P.R., 1990, Environmental assessments of industrial facilities or greenfield properties prior to acquisition, *Proceedings of 4th International Conference on Environmental Contamination, Barcelona, October 1990*.

3. Sanning, D.E. and Lewis, N.M., 1990, 1990 Update of the US Environmental Protection Agency's SITE Emerging Technology Program, *Journal of Air Waste Management Association*, 40 (12).
4. Travis, C.C. and Doty, C.B., 1990, Can contaminated aquifers at Superfund sites be remediated?, *Environmental Science Technology*, 24 (10).

6. *IN SITU* REMEDIATION USING VACUUM EXTRACTION TECHNIQUES

Gerald Licence

Vacuum extraction and dual vacuum extraction together form an innovative and cost effective cleanup technology. It was introduced in the USA and has now been developed for the UK market. This chapter describes the two operations, together with ways in which the technology can be combined with biological techniques. Other topics covered are monitoring for sub-surface leaks and the introduction of an environmental impairment liability insurance.

Vacuum extraction technology was first developed in 1984 in the United States of America by Terra Vac Incorporated. It is a simple technique — as shown in Figure 6.1, a system of screened wells is sunk within the polluted area of soil and linked to a vacuum pump; volatile or semi-volatile contaminants in the soil are drawn towards and up the wells. From there they can either be vented directly to the atmosphere, passed through an activated carbon filtration unit or fed into a catalytic oxidation unit and incinerated.

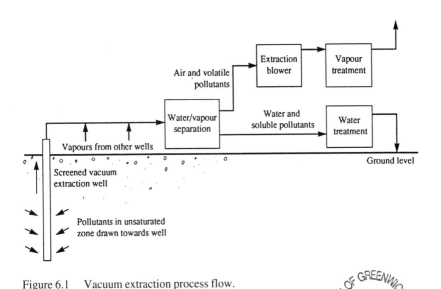

Figure 6.1   Vacuum extraction process flow.

TABLE 6.1
Representative contaminants

Volatiles	*Semi-Volatiles*

Volatiles
- acetone, benzene
- carbon tetrochloride
- chloroform
- cyclohexane, decane
- dichloroethylene (DCE)
- dimethylfuran
- ethyl acetate
- ethylbenzene, Freon 113
- hexane, methanol
- methyl ethyl ketone (MEK)
- methyl isobutyl ketone (MIBK)
- methyl methacrylate
- methylene chloride, pyridine
- tetrachloroethylene (PGE)
- tetrahydrofuran, toluene
- trichloroethane (TCA)
- trichloroethylene (TCE)
- xylenes

Semi-Volatiles
- chlorobenzene
- dichlorobenzene (DCB)
- trichloropane

Hydrocarbons
- diesel, gasoline
- heavy napthas
- jet fuel, kerosene
- Stoddard solvent

Inorganics
- ammonia

The technique has won widespread acceptance as the best *in situ*, on-site treatment for volatile and semi-volatile contaminants such as hydrocarbons and chlorinated solvents listed in Table 6.1. In 1987 the technique was favourably evaluated by the US Environmental Protection Agency under its SITE (Superfund Innovative Technology Evaluation) programme. Since then it has become one of the most widely used remediation techniques for hydrocarbons in the USA.

THE DEVELOPMENT OF DUAL VACUUM EXTRACTION
In its original form vacuum extraction is highly effective in removing volatile and semi-volatile contamination from the unsaturated layers of soil beneath a tank,

pipeline or building. By the time remediation measures begin, however, the spilled contamination has often percolated down into the sub-surface groundwater.

Pumping out the contaminated groundwater ('pump and treat') would appear to offer a straightforward method of *in situ* treatment. Unfortunately it merely deals with the effect of the contamination and not the cause. Contaminated groundwater may be endlessly pumped out and treated but unless something is done to remove the hydrocarbon pollution, it will continue to seep down into the groundwater. At best, 'pump and treat' applied in this way is merely an interim measure for containment. It is clearly much better to reduce the volume of hydrocarbon entering the groundwater by enlarging the unsaturated area of soil and tackling the contamination there.

This can be done by dual vacuum extraction (Figure 6.2). It works by deepening normal vacuum extraction wells so that they penetrate the groundwater table. The process has several advantages:

• It removes floating product (eg, diesel) from the groundwater table by gently lowering the table around each well, creating cones of depression down which the floating product flows before being drawn up and out through the wells.

• The dried out area around these cones of depression becomes amenable to vacuum extraction treatment; ie, to volatilization of the contamination.

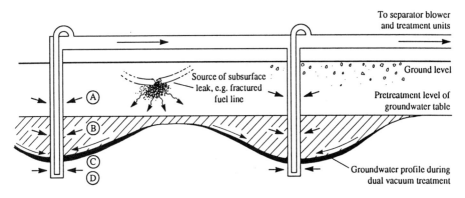

Figure 6.2   The principle of dual vacuum extraction. (A) Pollutant drawn from unsaturated soil towards wells; (B) Adsorbed pollutant in dried out 'cones of depression' ia also drawn towards wells; (C) Floating pollutant flows down surface of 'cones of depression' towards wells; (D) Pollutant in groundwater is drawn out through wells.

- It treats the 'smear zone', the area subject to seasonal or tidal fluctuations in the groundwater table where the heaviest contamination normally takes place.

CASE STUDIES

Dual vacuum extraction was the method used successfully to treat a sub-surface leak of more than 3,000 litres of diesel at the Texaco depot at Aberdeen in 1991. This depot had handled petrol, diesel, kerosene and gas oil for over 30 years and was to be sold as a going concern. A prior risk assessment study had identified the free-floating product as the prime risk. Accordingly excavation and disposal of the contaminated soils was felt to be too costly and inappropriate, whilst standard 'pump and treat' methods were rejected in view of the low levels of oil recovery and the unlikelihood of achieving a satisfactory standard of clean-up in a realistic period.

Since completing the project at Aberdeen, my company, Miller Environmental Limited (MEL), has undertaken a range of projects using vacuum extraction, dual vacuum extraction or a combination of the two. A co-ordinated approach which has been used successfully at several sites involves treating first the contamination in the unsaturated zone using vacuum extraction, then the floating product and the smear zone using dual vacuum extraction, and finally treating any residual contamination in the groundwater using 'pump and treat' techniques.

For example, at Burtonwood Motorway Services on the M62, MEL recently succeeded in remediating extensive sub-surface pollution using all three techniques together with a containment trench filled with Enviroclay — another MEL specialist technology.

COMBINED APPLICATIONS

The amenability of contamination to a specific *in situ* treatment depends on a variety of factors. In the case of sub-surface hydrocarbon pollution, the depth to groundwater, soil type and surface cover are all critical factors. Hydrocarbons which are lighter than diesel can be removed by direct vacuum extraction or dual vacuum extraction; heavier hydrocarbons are more amenable to bioremediation.

However, a combination of vacuum extraction and bioremediation can be most effective in certain situations. This is because the effect of drawing air through an area of soil contaminated by heavier hydrocarbons dramatically enhances the rate of biodegradation of the organic contaminants.

Even more effective is the removal and stockpiling of such contaminated material under waterproof sheeting and the application of vacuum extraction to these stockpiles through a series of pipes. Despite the double handling involved, this so-called *ex situ*/on-site technique can be cost effective.

In several cases, total petroleum hydrocarbon (TPH) levels have been reduced so effectively that soils removed from beneath old tanks and originally found to be too heavily impregnated with petroleum products to be acceptable for disposal to landfills, were subsequently found to be dry and acceptable after less than eight weeks of *ex situ*/on-site bioremediation enhanced by vacuum extraction.

VACUUM EXTRACTION AS A MONITORING SYSTEM

Within the last few months the issue of leaking underground storage tanks (LUST) has attracted much attention. Despite double-skinned tanks, shut-off valves and monitoring systems, leakages into the soil still occur. Specialist techniques for monitoring and containing these leaks are urgently required.

Practical experience with vacuum extraction as a soil treatment technique has shown that a network of vacuum extraction wells can also provide an effective monitoring system. Not only can the system monitor directly beneath large storage tanks, but it can also monitor associated underground pipes.

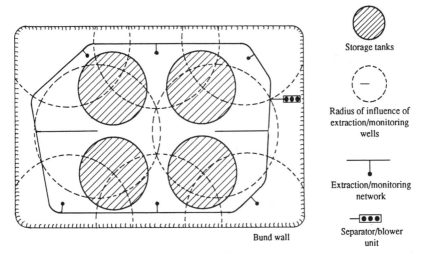

Figure 6.3   Vacuum extraction monitoring system at an oil storage depot.

It works like this. The wells are installed close to the tanks and/or alongside the pipes in such a way that the radius of influence of each well overlaps with that of the adjacent well. The system is operated automatically drawing air through the soil and monitoring the extracted soil vapour. If the TPH level rises above a preset maximum an alarm is triggered at the depot, filling station or (via a telemetric system) a central location. The vacuum extraction pump can then be switched on, preventing the leaked material spreading further through the soil.

Analysis and comparison of vapour readings from different wells in the overlapping system can assist in identifying the source and severity of the leak.

The advantage of such a system is that it can be installed at either a new or an existing petrol station, storage depot or process plant. It will detect material leaking directly beneath large tanks and requires no excavation or drilling beneath tanks, pipes or buildings — a particularly significant advantage at existing facilities where the risk of disturbing the subsoil beneath tanks or buildings could be severe.

ENVIRONMENTAL IMPAIRMENT LIABILITY INSURANCE

Environmental risks and financial liabilities arising from leaking underground storage tanks are a topical issue in petrochemical storage programmes. In the USA insurance claims arising from long-term leakages off site have created a situation in which environmental impairment liability (EIL) has become virtually impossible to obtain. Until September 1992, no satisfactory policy existed in the UK for underground storage tanks and pipes.

However, following evaluation of the vacuum extraction system, AIG Ltd, the largest insurance company in the world, together with Bowring Marsh & McLennan, one of the world's largest brokers, decided to offer an EIL policy based exclusively on the vacuum extraction monitoring system as installed by Miller Environmental Limited.

Initially aimed at the petrol station market, the policy has been recognized by Bowring Marsh & McLennan as having an obvious application for larger storage sites.

CONCLUSIONS

The combination of insurance, monitoring and treatment which I have described in this chapter offers an unprecedented degree of security to the owners and operators of petrochemical storage facilities. It is likely that similar comprehensive packages will become available over the next few years as landowners and developers attempt to minimize the risks associated with contaminated land.

The EIL policy which has been described has only been on offer for six months and it is therefore too early to judge its performance. However, the vacuum extraction remediation technology upon which it is based is well proven, and the monitoring system which has been developed from this technique is simple and effective.

REFERENCES

1. *US EPA Applications Analysis Report: Terra Vac In Situ Vacuum Extraction System EPA/540/A5-89/003.* Washington DC 1989.
2. Theile, P., Plaines, A. and Head, R., 1992, Vacuum extraction technology for the treatment of subsurface pollution — a case study, *IBC Conference on Contaminated Land — Policy and Regulation, February 1992.*
3. Theile, P., 1992, Vacuum extraction method of *in situ* cleaning of contaminated soil and polluted groundwater, *Proceedings of Second International Conference on Construction on Polluted and Marginal Land, July 1992.*
4. Licence, G., 1992, Cleanup technologies, *Proceedings of IBC Conference on Minimizing the Financial Risk of Acquiring, Owning, Constructing on or Remediating Contaminated Land, November 1992.*
5. Licence, G., 1992, Monitoring and treatment of petrochemical storage areas using vacuum extraction technology, *Proceedings of BSI Conference on Environmental Management and Maintenance of Hydrocarbon Storage Tanks, November 1992.*

7.   MOBILE INCINERATION
John Oesterle, Kathleen McNelis and Edward McVoy

Incineration has been identified by the United States Environmental Protection Agency (EPA) as the preferred remedial technology for most organic wastes in the USA. Management of the derelict wastes, as listed in the Superfund priority listings, is typically accomplished by a transportable, or mobile, incinerator.

The mobile incineration procedure has matured into a well-identified technology for remediation of hazardous and toxic waste sites in the USA. It is unique in component design for maximized space utilization, simplicity of operation and flexibility of control. These elements are part of the design as are transportability to US road standards, minimal mobilization/demobilization costs, and time for site change.

A state-of-the-art mobile system has recently been tested and con-firmed for use to remediate a waste chemical site in northern Ohio. The system is designed as a 65 peak million BTU per hour (144 kJ/hr) rotary kiln, vertical secondary, bag house and packed bed wet scrubber. This chapter explores design, shakedown and start-up needs, trial burn approaches and run data generated.

THE KINGSVILLE EXAMPLE.
The Kingsville, Ohio site (Figures 7.1, 7.2, 7.3) is an old gravel quarry in which industrial waste was deposited. During the remedial investigations (RI), toluene diisocyanate and diaminotoluene residues were identified as the principal waste constituents, with evidence of monochlorobenzene and monoethanolamine in the soils. Much of this waste was deposited in the landfill in drums. Initial estimates report (typically) 5,000 drums are located in the waste area. Volumes of waste estimated in government reports state 30,000 yd^3 (23,000 m^3) to be incinerated including the estimated 5,000 drums. Two principle organic hazardous constituents (POHCs) were used to qualify the Kingsville incinerator:

• monochlorobenzene ranked 19 for thermal stability;
• naphthalene ranked 5 for thermal stability.

Figure 7.1   Entrance to the Kingsville Superfund site.

Figure 7.2   Landfill excavation at the Kingsville site.

Figure 7.3   Barrels excavated from Kingsville landfill waiting shredding.

Utilization of these two POHCs was used as proof that all criteria would be met for both volatile and semi-volatile organics.

The Kingsville mobile incinerator system (Figure 7.4) was designed to maximum size constraints for over-the-road transport, and to a size which would provide for best economics, throughput and burn efficiency. As specified, the incinerator is an 8 ft (2.4 m) diameter, 40 ft (12.2 m) long rotary kiln designed for 35 million BTU/hr (77.5 kJ/hr) heat release. The total system heat release design is a maximum of 65 million BTU/hr (144 kJ/hr). Calculations for heat flow, residence times and waste material balance were used to provide credibility of the design to meet or exceed regulatory limits for solid and gaseous residues.

ESTABLISHMENT OF NEED OF MOBILE INCINERATION

The development of incineration procedures in the United States has been based on legislative dictates that hazardous waste must be destroyed to a health risk of 10^{-6} (one in one million) chance of adverse affect. For most remedial efforts, the only way to achieve this health risk base is through incineration. For the typical incineration scenario, the government has also stipulated destruction efficiency of at least 99.99% (as measured by destruction and removal efficiency (DRE)), gaseous emission controls for chlorine of 99.9%, limits for carbon monoxide (35 ppm) and nitrogen oxides (100 ppm) as well as particulate emissions of 0.08 grains/dry standard cubic foot (gr/dscf) (180 mg/dry standard cubic meter (dscm)). There are more details in Table 7.1.

To achieve waste destruction, waste has to be transported to the incinerator or the incinerator brought to the waste. Both approaches are highly controversial. However, because of the concerns over waste transport by road expressed by the agencies and the population, usual EPA directives specify on-site incineration. This is particularly true for waste sites larger than (typically) 3,000 tons. For incinerators to fit physically on these sites, given the small size and possible uneven terrain, designs must be mechanically flexible and take minimum planer area (footprint). The end result of these considerations constitutes the basis for the mobile incinerator.

BASIS OF DESIGN

The initiation of any designed function begins with the establishment of design restraints. This is also the case for a mobile incinerator. For example:

Figure 7.4   Mobile incinerator located at the Kingsville Ohio Superfund site.

TABLE 7.1

Potential performance criteria

Parameter	How it is measured	Limit
Destruction removal efficiency of organics	Mass flow of POHC is measured in incinerator feed (w_{in}) and in stack gas (w_{out}), then DRE is calculated: $$DRE = \frac{w_{in} - w_{out} \times 100}{w_{in}}.$$	99.99% minimum DRE some compounds require 99.99% minimum.
HCl emissions	Mass flow of Cl is measured in incinerator feed and HCl in stack gas.	The greater of 4 lb/hr limited or 99% removal of the stack gas.
	Sampled by isokinetic train (method 0050) or midget impinger (method 0051) ion chromatography (method 9057)*.	Limits depend on site specific conditions, terrain and stack height.
Particulate emissions	Particulate samples of stack gas as collected direct and weighed. Gas flowrates are adjusted to compare with the standard which is on a day basis converted to 7% O_2. There are some US state limits based on a certain percentage of CO_2 rather than O_2.	0.08 gr/dscf corrected to 7% O_2.
	Sampled and analysed by 40 cfr 60 methods 1 through 5.	0.08 gr/dscf corrected to 7% O_2.
Metals emissions	Before the incinerator is started up, modelling of the emission plume is performed (SCREEN, ISCST, ISCLT). This is used to predict areas of potential maximum impact. Air sampling equipment is placed at the locations shown to be impacted. Baseline samples are collected before start-up. Thereafter samples are collected and analysed on a scheduled basis.	Limits depend on the area and various US state and local requirements. Limits will usually be set by the regulating agency.
Ash and other solid residues	Samples are collected and analysed on a scheduled basis to show that pre-agreed set limits are being achieved.	Limits are usually set by the regulating agency.
Liquid effluent streams	As required to meet pre-agreed limits.	Limits are usually set by the regulating agency.

* Acceptable and certifiable chemical analytical methods offered by USEPA, defined in USEPA publication no 846.

• Each component must be capable of transport by road. In the USA maximum width restrictions are 13 ft (4 m), with permit, and height restrictions of 13 ft 6 in (4.11 m). Weight limitations vary, but are typically of the order of 13,000 lb (5897 kg) per load axle.

• Over-the-road maneuvering can be a real problem in getting to some waste sites. In some situations, it has been necessary to drive the flatbed wheels up onto grease-coated plywood and winch the flatbed around the curve. The USA does not have length restrictions (only axle weight). However, for these practical reasons, it has to be minimized. The longest truck section used for the system described here was 90 ft (27.5 m).

Once the system has been designed, boundary limits and methods of assembly must be considered. In a sense, all cables, conduits, duct work and so on are to be pre-fitted, heat-traced, and identified. This minimizes erection and start-up time. Electrical and control equipment — including, as necessary, an auxiliary power generator — is prepared as separate modules or skid-mounted mini-modules. Control room, motor control centre and personal facilities are also in a separate module, usually containing anti-vibration supports and air conditioning units.

Technical and/or thermal design of the mobile incinerator is based on heat and mass flow modelling with restraints learned from experience on certain flow parameters. Typically, US standard designs are restrained to:

• volumetric kiln fill no larger than 15%;

• kiln gas velocity (products of combustion) limited to 15 ft/s (4.6 m/s);

• kiln heat release 40,000 BTU/ft^3 (1133 BTU/m^3).

Each site must also be evaluated for additional restraints such as temperature of operation (ashing or slagging) and the propensity for forming dioxin and/or vaporizing metals.

THE MOBILE SYSTEM

PRIMARY COMBUSTION CHAMBER

The primary combustion chamber (Figure 7.5) is a refractory lined steel rotary kiln. Its overall length is 40 ft (12.2 m). The outside diameter of the kiln is 8 ft (2.44 m) and it is made of half inch thick steel. The kiln is lined with a 6 inch (12.24 cm) thickness of high alumina 3300°F (1815°C) rated refractory brick. The cross-sectional area of the inside of the kiln is 38.5 ft^2 (3.6 m^2) and it is driven by a 75 hp variable speed motor capable of rotating the kiln from 1 to

Figure 7.5   The Kingsville site. Note wheel hubs at the near end of the kiln.

4 rpm. The steel shell is reinforced with 6 inch wide bands of quarter inch (0.64 cm) plate at the trunions. Stainless steel Webbco Kiln leaflet model seals with graphite wear pads are used in both the front and back of the kiln.

HOT CYCLONE (Figure 7.6)

Gases enter the cyclone from the kiln. The cyclone serves as the primary source of particulate removal. Ducting connects the kiln exit, expands, then crosses in a 90° elbow and enters tangentially to the top of the cylindrical wall of the cyclone. The cyclone is flat-topped with an outside diameter of 8 ft and 2 inches (2.5 m). The cyclone contains 1 inch of mineral wool block insulation rated for 1900°F (1038°C) and 3.5 inches (8.9 cm) of low abrasion castable refractory rated for 2600°F (1427°C). Solids discharge from the cyclone to the wet ash drag conveyor. Combustion gases exit the cyclone through an inverted U-shaped ducting from the top of the cyclone to the secondary combustion chamber.

SECONDARY COMBUSTION CHAMBER

Gases enter the secondary combustion chamber (Figure 7.7) through duct work from the cyclone. The secondary combustion chamber (SCC) is a vertical up-fired chamber designed to operate up to 2200°F (1204°C). The gas residence

Figure 7.6   Hot cyclone used in the Kingsville system.

time is estimated at 3.5 seconds for the maximum gas flowrate of 62,500 actual cubic feet per minute (acfm) estimated for the lower BTU test case (1300 BTU/lb). The outside diameter of the SCC is 9 ft and 6 inches (2.9 m) of carbon steel plate. The secondary is lined with approximately 7 inches (17.8) of refractory. The inside diameter is 8 ft and 6 inches (2.6 m) for a cross-sectional area of approximately 57 ft^2 (5.27 m^2).

SPRAY DRYER

The spray dryer (Figure 7.7) serves as a quench chamber to lower the combustion gas temperature by addition of water. It consists of a 12 ft (3.65 m) outside diameter vertical retention chamber composed of a 63 ft and 6 inches (19.35 m) conical section which adjoins a tapered 45° conical section. Gases enter tangentially in the top of the chamber, pass through a gooseneck and travel downward through an atomized water spray. Scrubber water blowdown, injected at a temperature of 170–190°F (76.7–87.7°C) through a manifold assembly, is used as cooling water. Compressed air is used to atomize the water which is injected into the combustion gas through 7 nozzles.

BAG HOUSE

The bag house is a 20 module unit which houses 1,240 bags. Bags are 4.625 inches (11.7 cm) diameter by 8 ft (2.4 m) long made of 16 ounce (453 g) woven fibreglass with Teflon B finish. Collected particulate discharges to an auger for removal.

INDUCED DRAFT FAN

The induced draft fan is a radial blade centrifugal fan designed to induce a draft in the upstream components. The carbon steel fan is driven by a 250 HP/ 460 volt/3 phase motor rotating at 1800 rpm. The fan is designed to handle 40,000 acfm at 400°F (204°C) and 20.7 inches (52.6 cm) wc static pressure.

SCRUBBER/STACK

Quenched flue gases enter the packed tower absorber. The absorber is con-structed of fibreglass of a fire retardant grade with vinyl ester resin and is 9 ft (2.74 m) in diameter by approximately 25 ft (7.6 m) high. The scrubber contains 6 ft (1.8 m) of glass filled polypropylene packing, an integral recycle section, a spray header, and a Chevron type mist eliminator. The vessel is reinforced to

Figure 7.7   The Kingsville incinerator from the south end: left to right (1) wet scrubber and stack; (2) secondary combuster; (3) quench tower.

TABLE 7.2
Ash acceptance criteria

Constituent	Limit (mg/l)	Constituent	Limit (mg/l)
Barium	19	Tetra-chloroethane	0.095
Beryllium	0.019	Trans-1,2-dichlorethane	1.9
Chromium	0.95	Trichloroethane	0.095
Lead	1.9	Vinyl chloride	0.038
Monochlorobenzene	1.9	Polychlorinated	
Toluene-2,4-diamine	0.00171	biphenyls (PCBs)	2
Toluene-2,6-diamine	133	2, 3, 7, 8 Tetra-	
1,2 dichlorobenzene	11.4	chlorinated	
1,4 dichlorobenzene	1.425	dibenzo-p-dioxin (TCDD)	0.000015

support the integral stack.

ASH REMOVAL

The rotary kiln exit breaching is mated to a wet ash drag conveyor through a drop chute that extends downward into a water-filled ash drag basin. Solids from the rotary kiln drop under gravity to the ash drag water reservoir through this chute. A discharge chute from the cyclone also extends down into the ash drag basin for collection of cyclone solids. The kiln discharge breaching chute and the cyclone discharge chute are submerged below the water level in the ash drag, thereby creating a water seal and preventing air leakage into the system. Ash from these two sources will freely fall through the water and deposit onto the ash drag conveyor flighting.

The ash is dragged through the water and up an inclined slope, rising above the water line allowing the ash to drain the water back into the reservoir. Ash is conveyed to temporary storage until it can be tested prior to transfer to the main storage area. Acceptance testing of the ash is by the toxic characteristic leaching procedure (TCLP) with measurements as shown in Table 7.2.

CONTROL CONCEPTS

The control system for the Kingsville incinerator is a PC-based digital control system (Figure 7.8). The system is composed of two interchangeable computers, one serving as the system control and the other as the data monitor. For normal operations these two units act in a master-slave arrangement. A redundant file data storage system is provided to both computers. Component and data links are provided by NOVEL software.

Strategy of control is in an icon format where each control parameter is treated as a separate building block. Control resides in the 'control' PC which provides field responsive changes by sending a control signal to a field converter which produces a 4–20 ma output for control.

The overall system is interchangeable between the control master and the slave monitoring computer. In the event of PC (control) failure, the field devices hold their last position until the slave is brought down, file data restored and the monitor computer is returned to line as the control PC. This switch-over takes approximately 1 minute.

Site arrangement for the control system is shown in Figure 7.9 overleaf.

The control parameters that are required by the regulatory agencies are:

- kiln exit temperature;
- kiln draft;
- excess oxygen at the secondary combustion chamber exit;
- secondary combustion chamber exit temperature;

Figure 7.8   Control panels for the Kingsville incinerator.

- stack oxygen;
- stack carbon dioxide;
- corrected carbon monoxide;
- combustion efficiency;
- scrubber pH.

The regulatory agencies are mainly concerned that the waste is destroyed using good combustion principles. Figures 7.10, 7.11, 7.12 and 7.13 are examples of operating performance.

Most of the instrumentation is dedicated to the control of the combustion process. There are thermocouples at the inlet and exit of the kiln. The thermocouples are used to adjust the combustion zone as close as possible to the inlet breaching. Kiln exit oxygen is also a monitored parameter. The oxygen is monitored to assure there is enough excess oxygen in the kiln for adequate combustion of the waste. The natural gas and air are controlled separately to allow the addition of either gas or air as needed. The SCC exit and spray dryer inlet temperatures are also monitored. If there is a dramatic temperature difference, there is either an air leak or an instrumentation calibration problem.

Figure 7.9   Location of the control house for the Kingsville operation.

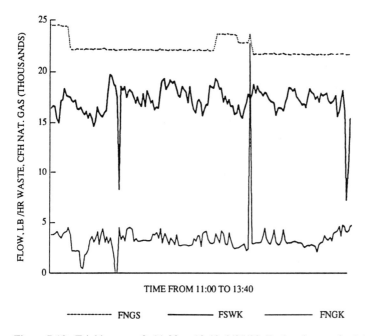

FLOW, LB /HR WASTE, CFH NAT. GAS (THOUSANDS)

TIME FROM 11:00 TO 13:40

------------ FNGS ———— FSWK ———— FNGK

Figure 7.10   Trial burn no. 2, 11.00 to 13.40, 9/25/92. Fuel and waste feed; kiln and secondary. FNGS Fuel flow of natural gas to secondary; FSWK Fuel from solid waste to kiln; FNGK Fuel flow of natural gas to kiln.

The spray dryer water flow and pressure, along with the atomizing air pressure, are the control parameters for the temperature control. A characterization table was developed based on the nozzle curves. The spray dryer temperature is a redundant thermocouple. The baghouse must be maintained between 450 and 500°F (232 and 260°C). If it goes too low, there is a potential for HCl condensation, and if the temperature is too high, the bags may be scorched.

The main parameters that are controlled on the air pollution control train are the baghouse differential pressure, ID fan amps, ID fan vibration, quench water flow, packed tower recirculation flow and stack temperature, along with pH and the stack gases. The stack gases are monitored using a heated probe in the stack and an extractive analyser system. All of the corrections and the combustion efficiencies are calculated in the control PCs.

Any of the parameters listed above will cause the waste feed to be terminated. All conditions must be within the specified operating range to allow

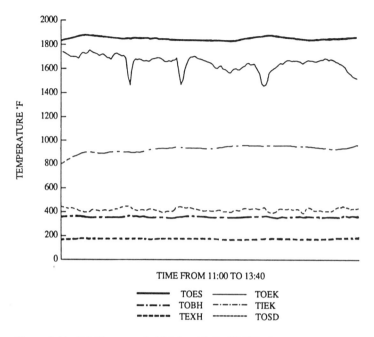

TIME FROM 11:00 TO 13:40

——— TOES	——— TOEK
—·—·— TOBH	—··—··— TIEK
——————— TEXH	---------- TOSD

Figure 7.11 Trial burn no. 2, 11.00 to 13.40, 9/25/92. Operating temperatures. TOES Temperature outlet end of secondary; TOEK Temperature outlet end of kiln; TIEK Temperature inlet end of kiln; TOSD Temperature outlet of spray dryer; TOBH Temperature outlet of baghouse; TEXH Temperature exhaust.

waste feed to be initiated and to continue. Waste is terminated automatically and cannot be reinstated until the parameters are back within acceptable limits.

Arrangement of the control module can be seen in Figure 7.8, page 131.

INCINERATION TEST CRITERIA

The EPA has standardized minimum test criteria for all hazardous waste incinerators (Table 7.1, page 125). For the most part, the criteria are based on waste destruction level acceptable to health risk standards; usually 10^{-6} probability of adverse health effects. For flexibility and to allow individual states participation, the EPA allowed each state the prerogative of writing its own regulation provided it met the federal criteria. Most states accepted the federal regulation verbatim. Those states that did not, generally accepted most of the federal regulations and tightened specific parameters to fit their own needs. The more typical parameters added by individual states are:

• Reduction of particulate emissions from 0.08 gr/dscf to 0.01 gr/dscf (or less).

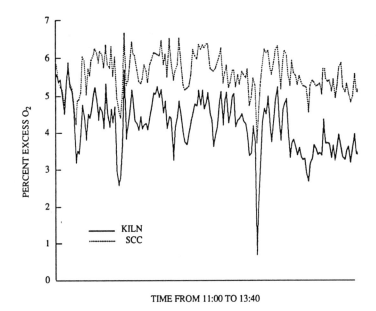

Figure 7.12   Trial burn no. 2, 11.00 to 13.40, 9/25/92. Excess O_2 kiln and secondary.

• 2,3,7,8-dioxin is sometimes added as an acceptance criteria. Typically a limit of 5 ppb defines dioxin emissions. Some states also added dioxin limits to solid residues with acceptance criteria in the order of 5 ppt.

• Added heavy metals to the emission criteria, principally Cr^{6+}, Pb, As, Hg, Ni. These are typically contained in regulations developed for boilers and industrial furnaces (BIF codes).

The performance criteria are set prior to design and become part of the design basis. These criteria stipulate limits which will apply to emissions and characteristics of ash and other residues.

Performance requirements mandated for the Kingsville site for stack emissions are as follows:

• 99.99% DRE;

• HCl <4 lb/hr;

• particulate <0.08 gr/dscf;

• combustion efficiency 99%.

The principle test parameter used by the agency to define system acceptability is DRE (destruction and removal efficiency). DRE for most

135

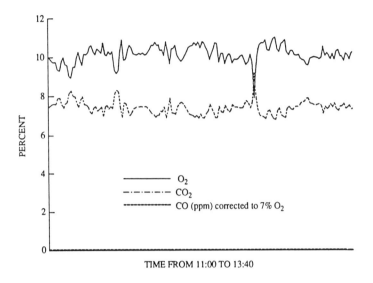

Figure 7.13   Trial burn no. 2, 11.00 to 13.40, 9/25/92. Stack gas O_2, CO_2 and corrected CO.

hazardous waste products is 99.99%; DRE for toxic materials is six 9s, or 99.9999% removal.

DRE is a measurement made on gaseous emissions being exhausted through the stack. For the purpose of providing a statistically significant test for DRE, virgin organic compounds with known levels of thermal destructibility are used as surrogate spikes in the waste stream. Generally, selection of surrogates (called POHCs for principle organic hazardous constituents) is made based on the more difficult compounds to incinerate. For the Kingsville system, two surrogates were used: a volatile monochlorobenzene and a semi-volatile compound — naphthalene. Feed concentrations equal to 1% of the waste feed rate (10,000 ppm) are used for test purposes to provide adequate test significance.

On completion of test burns and their acceptability to regulated criteria, the facility was authorized to commence production incineration.

CONCLUSIONS FROM TEST BURNS
Pertinent data summary from the Kingsville incinerator test is summarized in Table 7.3. These data support the contention that the Kingsville incinerator has met all appropriate criteria of 40 CFR 264 Subpart O, Ambient Air Quality

TABLE 7.3
Selected test burn data

Condition 1	1	2	3
Solid waste feed rate	9.0 T/H	8.5 T/H	8.7 T/H
Kiln temperature outlet	1670°F	1700°F	1700°F
Kiln temperature inlet	940°F	1100°F	1150°F
XS O_2 kiln	6%	5.5%	4%
OS O_2 secondary	6%	4%	5.5%
DRE MCB*	99.9 est	99.99 est	99.99 est
DRE naphthalene	99.999	99.998	99.998
Hydrogen chloride	0.0149 L/H	0.0186 L/H	0.0280 L/H
Particulate (gr/dscf)	0.00173	0.00192	0.00121

* MCB samples cross contaminated

Condition 1	1	2	3
Solid waste feed rate	12.5 T/H	12.5 T/H	12.5 T/H
Kiln temperature outlet	1690°F	1600°F	1500°F
Kiln temperature inlet	1150°F	1150°F	1200°F
XS O_2 kiln	5.5%	4.5%	5.5%
OS O_2 secondary	5.5%	4.5%	5.5%
DRE MCB	99.9999%	99.9999%	99.9999%
DRE naphthalene	99.9997%	99.9990%	99.9991%
Hydrogen chloride	0.0346 L/H	0.0365 L/H	0.0656 L/H
Particulate (gr/dscf)	0.00217	0.00634	0.00315

Standards and Air Toxic Limits.
    Production release will continue as follows:

- heat input from waste feed 35,000,000 BTU/hr;
- maximum kiln lead and temperature 1750°F (954°C);
- maximum feed rate 12 tph.

START-UP
The combination of clay concentration and moisture created some additional

137

problems with solid waste feed. Even with a 15° slope on the sidewalls of the feed hoppers, bridging occurred in both. The simplest and most economical remedy for bridging was a rod-out by operating personnel. Remote TV monitoring was used to minimize the occurrence. As a matter of note, heavy duty bin vibrators did little to elevate the bridges. While this approach may be rather archaic, bear in mind that the tenure on site is estimated at one year. This effort can support an extra man on staff as opposed to stopping to redesign the feed system with the associated physical and labour costs.

Starting problems are familiar on most large mechanical systems. In the case of the Kingsville incinerator, most were related to characteristics of the waste and its effect on the drive system. The single most difficult problem to resolve was with the auger feed. Packing characteristics of the waste produced high levels of torsional load on the auger shaft eventually leading to fatigue failure of the shaft. Re-alignment of hanger bearings eased the fatigue problem but transferred stress to the drive components. Eventually the drive failed. At this time, the auger assembly was re-configured. Little or no problems have been encountered since.

PRODUCTION

All hazardous waste incineration production within the United States is based solely on pre-qualified destruction parameters. These parameters, as discussed above, limit waste heat values, feed rate and kiln temperature. Using these parameters, prior testing has shown compliance to destruction criteria.

At the time of this presentation, the Kingsville facility is in the fifth month (of 12) of production. To date, it has been a routine burn; DRE of five to six 9s, ash has met all criteria, including dioxin, and particulate has been well below specifications.

Normal operation of the incinerator calls for a 3 shift, 24 hour, 7 day continuous operation. This is met by four staffed shifts each working 8 hours over the length of the project (one shift is always off) with each shift working a 48 hour week. An alternate shift schedule has been three 12 hour shifts with alternate 3 and 4 days off per week.

The typical labour loading is three people per shift with daylight having primary responsibility for maintenance and management. The three regular individuals per shift consist of the following:

• one system qualified operator;
• one assistant operator;
• one field helper.

During start-up and testing, this manpower arrangement is usually increased to 4 to 5 people to provide assistance for system evaluation and to record specific data required by the agencies.

Record keeping during all test periods and into production are directed by agency protocol as the direct means of determining the acceptability of the remedial efforts. These file data support all claims of waste burning performance.

MATERIAL PREPARATION

Excavation of the landfill provided the usual surprises; that is, municipal trash was obviously deposited in the landfill along with the chemical wastes. Usual items such as tyres, bed springs and washing machines are the type of waste uncovered.

Excavated waste and soils have a number of features which must be controlled in order to provide acceptable combustion. Paramount of these features is uniformity of heat value. This obviously includes moisture content since water has a direct, deleterious effect on operating temperature. Obviously, if temperature is not maintained, the destruction of the target waste organic(s) can be affected. In addition, barrel shards, rocks, scrap tyres, etc must be either removed from the waste stream or reduced in size so that they can be fed through the auger.

For the Kingsville system, it was decided to use two size reducing units: one a low energy rotating shear shredder ('saturn' type), and the second a high energy flail type reducer. In combination, these two size reducers can account for the average waste products, excluding large rocks and concrete. These combinations will also prepare personal protective equipment such as 'Tyvek' for burning.

Within reason, the material preparation sequence (flail homogenizer) worked well on the dry (less than 15% moisture). In the combination of high moisture (in the order of 25% and above) and clay, clay balls would be passed through the flail in sizes up to 3–4 inches (7–10 cm).

The combination of high clay and high moisture created other concerns during the actual burn. The clay balls would bake and be carried into the ash pile as hard, ceramic balls. Fortunately, open porosity in the ball would allow escape of organic vapours.

High clay, rocks and other debris, including drum shards, put size constraints on everything entering the feed system. The preferred system for solids is a double (side by side) auger system, providing sufficient room is available on the face plate.

Liquid waste feed was designed to be a 'drip' into the waste feed hopper. This arrangement provides for a controlled entry into the incinerator with minimal risk of adverse temperature control. Transfer of waste liquids and sludges is handled by diaphragm pumps through a line-of-sight pipe into a pressure plenum, with a drip going into the solids feed hopper. This arrangement is very effective in handling waste liquids and sludges.

PERFORMANCE CRITERIA

Ash acceptance criteria are shown in Table 7.2 on page 130.

SUMMARY

The incineration of site wastes at Kingsville is being conducted in conformance with operational protocols shown as being acceptable by preliminary testing. The margin of acceptability of these test data and of the production overcheck serves to show statistically that site remediation will meet health risk criteria as measured by regulated parameters. It is expected that remediation of the Kingsville site will continue through all aspects of closure without major perturbations.